Rise, Let Us Be
On Our Way

JOHN PAUL II

RISE, LET US BE ON OUR WAY

JONATHAN CAPE
LONDON

Published by Jonathan Cape 2004

Previously published in the Polish language as *Wstańcie, chodźmy!*

2 4 6 8 10 9 7 5 3 1

This Jonathan Cape edition is published by arrangement with Arnoldo Mondadori Editore S.p.A.,
20090 Segrate, Milan, Italy

First published in Great Britain in 2004 by
Jonathan Cape
Random House, 20 Vauxhall Bridge Road, London SW1V 2SA

Random House Australia (Pty) Limited
20 Alfred Street, Milsons Point, Sydney,
New South Wales 2061, Australia

Random House New Zealand Limited
18 Poland Road, Glenfield,
Auckland 10, New Zealand

Random House South Africa (Pty) Limited
Endulini, 5A Jubilee Road, Parktown 2193, South Africa

The Random House Group Limited Reg. No. 954009
www.randomhouse.co.uk

A CIP catalogue record for this book is available from the British Library

ISBN 0-224-07590-X

Papers used by Random House are natural,
recyclable products made from wood grown in sustainable forests;
the manufacturing processes conform to the environmental
regulations of the country of origin

Book design by L&G McRee

Printed and bound in Great Britain by
Clays Ltd, St Ives plc

CONTENTS

INTRODUCTION

When *Gift and Mystery* was published—the book that recounted my memories and reflections on the early years of my priesthood—I received many messages, especially from young people, saying how much they liked the book.[1] I was given to understand that for many of them, this personal supplement to the Apostolic Exhortation *Pastores Dabo Vobis* served as a valuable aid in helping them discern their own personal vocations. This made me very happy. May Christ continue to use those reflections so that many young people will hear His invitation: *"Come, follow me, and I will make you fishers of men" (Mark 1:17).*

On the occasion of the forty-fifth anniversary of my ordination as a bishop and the twenty-fifth anniversary of my election as the successor of Saint Peter, I was asked to write a sequel to those recollections, beginning with the year 1958 when I was named a bishop. I felt it was right to accept this suggestion as I had done for my earlier book. An added motive to collect and arrange these memories and reflections was the work that had taken place on a document about the episcopal ministry—the Apostolic Exhortation *Pastores Gregis*. In that document I presented a synthesis of the ideas that emerged from the Tenth Ordinary General Assembly of the Synod of Bishops, which took place the day after the Great Jubilee of the Year 2000. As I listened to the presentations in the Synod Hall and later read the propositions that were presented to me, I recalled the years during which I served the Church in Kraków as well as many new situations I have experienced in Rome as the successor of Saint Peter.

I wanted to put these thoughts in writing, so as to share with others these signs of the love of Christ, who throughout the ages has been calling new successors of the Apostles so as to pour forth His grace, through earthenware vessels, into the hearts of others. The words of Saint Paul to the young bishop Timothy were constantly echoing in my mind: *"He has redeemed us and called us with a holy calling, not in virtue of our works, but in virtue of his own purpose and the grace which was granted to us in Christ Jesus before this world existed"* (2 Tim. 1:9).

I offer this book as a sign of love to my brother

bishops and to all the People of God. May it help all who wish to learn about the greatness of the episcopal ministry, the difficulty associated with it, but also about the joy that daily accompanies its fulfillment. I invite all to offer with me a Te Deum of praise and thanksgiving. With our gaze fixed on Christ, strengthened by hope that does not disappoint, let us journey together along the paths of the new millennium: *"Rise, let us be on our way!" (cf. Mark 14:42).*

VOCATION

"You did not choose me, but I chose you" (John 15:16)

The Source of My Vocation

I set off in search of the source of my vocation. It is beating there . . . in the Upper Room in Jerusalem. I thank God that during the Great Jubilee of the Year 2000 I was able to pray—precisely there—in the *Upper Room (Mark 14:15)*, where the Last Supper took place. I transport myself in thought to that memorable Thursday, when Christ, *having loved his own to the end (cf. John 13:1)*, instituted the Apostles as priests of the New Covenant. I see Him bending down before each of us, successors of the Apostles, to wash our feet. I hear Him, as if He were speaking to me—to us—these words: *"Do you realize what I have done for you? You call me 'Teacher' and 'Master,' and rightly so, for indeed I am. If I, therefore, the master and teacher, have washed your* feet, you ought also to wash one another's feet. I have given you an example to follow, so that as I have done for you, you also should do" (John 13:12–16).

Together with Peter, Andrew, James, and John . . . let us continue to listen: "As the Father has loved me, so I have loved you. Remain in my love! If you keep my commandments, you will remain in my love, just as I have kept my Father's commandments and remain in his love. I have told you this so that my joy might be in you and your joy might be complete. This is my commandment: love one another as I have loved you. No one has greater love than this, to lay down one's life for one's friends. You are my friends if you do what I command you" (John 15:9–14).

Is not the *mysterium caritatis* of our vocation contained in these sayings? These words of Christ, spoken *at the hour for which he had come (cf. John 12:27),* are at the root of every vocation in the Church. From them flows the life-giving sap that nourishes every vocation: those of the Apostles and their successors, but also every other vocation, because the Son wishes to be a friend to everyone: because He gave His life for all. Here we find what is most important, most valuable, and most sacred: the love of the Father and the love of Christ for us, His and our joy, and also our friendship and fidelity, which express themselves in the fulfillment of the commandments. These words also contain the goal and the meaning of our vocation: to *"go and bear fruit that will last"* (John 15:16).

The bond of love unites all things; substantially it

unites the Divine Persons, but on a different level it also unites human beings and their different vocations. We have entrusted our life to Christ, who loved us first and, as the Good Shepherd, offered His life for us. The Apostles heard Christ's words and applied them to themselves as their personal vocation. So too we, their successors, shepherds of Christ's Church, cannot but feel impelled to be the first to respond to this love, faithfully fulfilling the commandments and offering our life every day for the friends of our Lord.

"The good shepherd lays down his life for the sheep" (John 10:11). In the homily I preached in Saint Peter's Square on October 16, 2003, on the occasion of the twenty-fifth anniversary of my pontificate, I said: "While Jesus was saying these words, the Apostles did not realize that he was referring to himself. Not even his beloved Apostle John knew it. He understood on Calvary, at the foot of the Cross, when he saw Jesus silently giving up his life for 'his sheep.' When the time came for John and the other Apostles to assume this same mission they then remembered his words. They realized that they would be able to fulfill their mission only because he had assured them that he himself would be working among them."[2]

"You did not choose me, but I chose you and appointed you to go and bear fruit that will last" (John 15:16). Not you, but I!—says Christ. This is the foundation of the efficacy of a bishop's pastoral mission.

The Call

The year is 1958. I'm on a train traveling toward Olsztyn with my group of canoeists. We are beginning the vacation schedule that we have been following since 1953: part of the vacation we are to spend in the mountains, most often in the Bieszczady mountains, and part on the lakes in the Masuria region. Our destination is the Łyna River. That's why—it is July—we are on the train bound for Olsztyn. I say to the so-called admiral—as far as I can remember at that time it was Zdzisław Heydel: "Zdzisław, I'm going to have to leave the canoe because I have been summoned by the Primate [since the death of Cardinal August Hlond in 1948, Cardinal Stefan Wyszyński was the Primate] and I must go to see him."

The admiral said: "That's fine, I'll see to it."

And so, when the time came, we left the group to go to the nearest railroad station, at Olsztynek.

Knowing that I would have to see the Primate during our time on the Łyna River, I had deliberately left my good cassock with friends in Warsaw. It wouldn't be right to visit the Primate wearing the old cassock I brought along on our canoe trips (on such trips I always brought a cassock and a complete set of vestments so that I could celebrate Mass).

So I set off, first in the canoe over the waves of the river, and then in a truck laden with sacks of flour, until I got to Olsztynek. The train for Warsaw left late at night. I had brought my sleeping bag with me, thinking that I might be able to catch a few winks in the station and ask someone to wake me when it was time to board the train. There was no need for that in any event, because I didn't sleep.

In Warsaw I arrived on Miodowa Street at the specified hour. There I discovered that three other priests had also been summoned: Father Wilhelm Pluta from Silesia, Father Michał Blecharczyk, pastor of Bochnia in the diocese of Tarnów, and Father Józef Drzazga from Lublin. At first I paid no attention to this coincidence. Only later did I realize that they had been summoned for the same reason as I.

As I entered the office of the Primate, he told me that the Holy Father had named me an auxiliary bishop to the archbishop of Kraków. In February of that same year (1958) Bishop Stanisław Rospond had died. He had been auxiliary bishop of Kraków for many years during the reign of the prince archbishop of Kraków, Cardinal Adam Sapieha.

Upon hearing the words of the Primate informing me of the decision of the Holy See, I said, "Your Eminence, I am too young; I'm only thirty-eight."

But the Primate said, "That is a weakness which can soon be remedied. Please do not oppose the will of the Holy Father."

So I said, "I accept."

"Then let's have lunch," the Primate concluded.

He invited all four of us to lunch. There I found out that Father Wilhelm Pluta had been named bishop of Gorzów Wielkopolski. At that time it was the largest Apostolic Administration in Poland. It encompassed Szczecin and Kołobrzeg, one of the oldest dioceses in Poland, which had been created in the year 1000 (at the same time, Gniezno became the metropolitan see of the province, which included not only Kołobrzeg, but also Kraków and Wrocław). Father Józef Drzazga was named auxiliary bishop of Lublin (later he was transferred to Olsztyn), and Father Michał Blecharczyk was named auxiliary bishop in Tarnów.

At the conclusion of this audience, of such great importance for my life, I realized that I could not return immediately to my canoeing friends: first I had to go to

Kraków to inform Archbishop Eugeniusz Baziak, my Ordinary. While waiting for the night train to Kraków, I spent many hours in prayer at the chapel of the Ursuline Sisters in Warsaw on Wiślana Street.

Archbishop Baziak, the Latin rite metropolitan of Lviv, suffered the fate of all displaced persons: He was forced to leave Lviv. He settled in Lubaczów, that little corner of the archdiocese of Lviv that remained on the Polish side of the boundaries established at Yalta. Prince Adam Sapieha, archbishop of Kraków, asked a year before he died that Archbishop Baziak, having been forced to leave his own diocese, might become his coadjutor. This is how my own episcopate is chronologically linked with the person of this sorely tested Prelate.

The next day I went to see Archbishop Eugeniusz Baziak at 3 Franciszkańska Street and handed him a letter from the Cardinal Primate. I remember it as if it were today. The Archbishop took me by the arm and led me into the waiting room where there were priests sitting, and he said: *"Habemus papam"*—"We have a Pope." In the light of subsequent events, one might say that these words were prophetic.

When I said to the Archbishop that I would like to return to Masuria to join my friends who were canoeing on the Łyna River, he answered: "I don't think that would be appropriate."

Somewhat troubled by this reply, I went to the

Church of the Franciscans and prayed the Way of the Cross. I often went there for this purpose because the stations are original, modern, painted by Józef Mehoffer. Then I went back to Archbishop Baziak renewing my request. I said, "I appreciate your concern, Excellency, but I would still ask you to allow me to return to Masuria."

This time he answered: "Yes, yes, by all means. But I ask you, please," he added with a smile, "come back in time for the consecration."

So that very evening I again boarded the train for Olsztyn. I had with me Hemingway's book *The Old Man and the Sea*. I read it all night. Once I dozed off. I felt somewhat strange . . .

When I arrived at Olsztyn, my group was already there. They had canoed down the Łyna River. The admiral came for me to the station and said, "So, did Uncle become a bishop?"

To this I said yes. He said: "That is exactly what I imagined in my heart, and what I wished for you."

As a matter of fact, shortly beforehand, on the occasion of my tenth anniversary of ordination, he had wished me this. When I was named a bishop, I was hardly twelve years a priest.

I had slept little. When I reached my destination, I was tired. First, however, before going to rest, I went to church to celebrate Mass. The church was under the care of the university chaplain, Father Ignacy

Tokarczuk, who was later named a bishop. After a short rest, I awoke and realized that the news had already spread, because Father Tokarczuk said to me: "Oh, the new bishop. Congratulations."

I smiled and went to join my canoeing friends. When I took the paddle, I again felt somewhat strange. The coincidence of dates struck me: The date of my nomination was July fourth, the anniversary date of the blessing of Wawel Cathedral. It is an anniversary that I have always cherished in my heart. I thought this coincidence must have some special meaning. I also thought maybe this was the last time I could go canoeing. Later though, I should mention, it turned out that there were many opportunities for me to go swimming and canoeing on the rivers and lakes of Masuria. As a matter of fact, I continued until the year 1978.

Successor of the Apostles

After the summer vacation I returned to Kraków to begin preparations for the consecration, which was set for September twenty-eighth, the feast of Saint Wenceslaus, patron of Wawel Cathedral. This dedication is evidence of the historical ties between Poland and Bohemia. Saint Wenceslaus was a Bohemian count who lost his life as a martyr at the hands of his own brother. The Czechs also venerate him as their patron.

An essential part of the preparation for my episcopal ordination was the retreat. I made it at Tyniec, an historic abbey I often visited. This time the stay was especially important for me. I was to become a bishop. I was already nominated. I still had some time before the consecration—more than two months. I had to make use of the time in the best way possible.

The retreat lasted six days—six days of meditation. Dear Lord, what an abundance of fruit! "Successor of the Apostles"—at that time I heard these very words from the lips of a physicist I knew. Obviously, believers attach great importance to the apostolic succession. I, a successor, thought with great humility of the Apostles of Christ and of this long, unbroken chain of bishops who, by the laying on of hands, passed on to their successors a share in the Apostolic Office. Now they were to bestow it upon me. I felt personally linked to each of them. Many of those who preceded the current generation of bishops in this chain of succession we know by name. In some cases their pastoral activities are also known and acclaimed. But even in the case of the bishops of antiquity, unknown today, their episcopal vocation and work continues—*"that your fruit will last" (John 16:16)*. This happens partly through us, their successors. Precisely through their hands and by virtue of the efficacy of the sacrament, we are joined to Christ, who chose both them and us *"before the foundation of the world" (Eph. 1:4)*. Wonderful gift and mystery!

"Ecce sacerdos magnus qui in diebus suis placuit Deo. . . . Ideo iureiurando fecit illum Dominus crescere in plebem suam" . . . thus we sing in the liturgy. This one high priest of the new and eternal covenant is Jesus Christ Himself. He consummated the sacrifice of His priest-

hood by dying on the cross, offering His life for His sheepfold—all of mankind. It was He who instituted the sacrament of priesthood during the Last Supper on the day before He shed His blood in the sacrifice offered on the Cross. It was He who took bread into His hands and said these words: *"This is my body which will be given up for you."* It was He who later, taking into His hands the cup filled with wine, said these words: *"This is my blood of the new and everlasting covenant which will be shed for you and for all so that sins may be forgiven."* And at the end He added: *"Do this in memory of me."* He said this in the presence of the Apostles, in the presence of the Twelve, of whom Peter is the first. He said to them: *"Do this in memory of me."* In this way He made them priests in His own likeness, the one high Priest of the New Covenant.

As participants in the Last Supper, maybe the Apostles didn't fully understand what these words meant—words that would be fulfilled the next day when the body of Christ was sentenced to be crucified, and his blood was shed on the Cross. Perhaps at the time they understood only that they were to reenact the rite of the Supper with bread and wine. The Acts of the Apostles recall that the first Christians, after these paschal events, devoted themselves *"to the breaking of the bread and to prayer" (Acts 2:42)*. By then, the meaning of the rite was already clear to all.

In the liturgy of the Church, Holy Thursday is the

day we recall the Last Supper, the institution of the Eucharist. From the Upper Room in Jerusalem, the celebration of the Eucharist gradually spread to the whole known world. In the beginning, the Apostles presided at the Eucharist in Jerusalem. Later, as the Gospel spread, it was celebrated both by the Apostles and by those upon whom they had laid hands—in ever new places, beginning with Asia Minor. Finally, with Saint Peter and Saint Paul, the Eucharist reached Rome, the capital of the contemporary world. Centuries later it reached the Vistula River.

I remember that during my retreat before my episcopal ordination I thanked God in a special way that the Gospel and the Eucharist had reached the Vistula River, and that they had also reached the abbey at Tyniec. This abbey, south of Kraków, whose beginnings date back to the eleventh century, was the proper place to prepare myself for my episcopal ordination in Wawel Cathedral. When I visited Kraków in 2002, before returning to Rome, I was able to visit Tyniec, even if only briefly. It was a special payment of a personal debt of gratitude. I owe so much to Tyniec. Perhaps not only I, but all of Poland.

September 28, 1958, was slowly approaching. Before the ceremony, as a newly named bishop, I visited Lubaczów for the celebration of the silver jubilee of Archbishop Baziak's episcopate. It was the Feast of Our Lady of Sorrows, which in Lviv was celebrated on September twenty-second. I was there with two bishops from Przemyśl: Bishop Franciszek Barda and Bishop Wojciech Tomaka—both old men, and I, a youthful thirty-eight-year-old. I felt embarrassed. That is where I had my first "trial run" for the episcopate. A week later the consecration took place at Wawel Cathedral.

Wawel

From childhood I have had a very special bond with Wawel Cathedral. I don't remember my first visit there, but from the time I began to visit the cathedral, I felt particularly spellbound and personally attached to it. In some way, Wawel encompasses the whole of Poland's history. I lived through the tragic period when the Nazi governor Hans Frank took up quarters in Wawel Castle, and a flag with a swastika flew over it. For me this was a particularly painful experience. But there came a day when the flag with the swastika disappeared, and the Polish flag returned.

The present cathedral dates back to the time of Casimir the Great. I remember and recall every corner of this shrine and all of its monuments. As you walk through the main nave and the side aisles, you see the sarcophagi of Polish kings. And when you descend to the crypt of the poets, you come upon the graves of Mickiewicz, Słowacki, and finally Norwid.

As I mentioned in *Gift and Mystery*, I had wanted very much to offer my first Mass at Wawel, in the crypt of Saint Leonard underneath the cathedral. And so it was. No doubt this desire came from my deep love for everything redolent of the spirit of my homeland. This place in which every stone speaks of Poland, and of its greatness, is very dear to me. The whole of the Wawel complex is dear to me: the cathedral, the castle, and the courtyard. The last time I was in Kraków, I visited Wawel and prayed before the tomb of Saint Stanislaus. I could not omit a visit to the cathedral where I had spent twenty years.

My favorite place in Wawel Cathedral is the crypt of Saint Leonard. It is part of the old cathedral, which goes back to the time of Boleslaus III, known as the Wrymouth. The crypt itself bears witness to an even earlier period. It dates from the time of the first bishops in the early eleventh century, when the Krakowian epis-copal line began. These first bishops have mysterious names like Prokop and Prokulf, as if of Greek back-ground. Gradually there appear new names, now more often of Slavic origin, like Stanislaus of Szczepanów, who became bishop of Kraków in 1072. In 1079 he was murdered by men dispatched by King Boleslaus II, the

Bold. Later this king had to flee the country and supposedly lived out his life in penance in Osjak. When I became the metropolitan of Kraków, on my return from Rome, I offered Mass in Osjak. It was there that I drafted a poem about this event that took place so many centuries earlier, entitled "Stanislaus."

Saint Stanislaus, "Father of our homeland." On the Sunday after May eighth, there is a great procession from Wawel to Skałka. All the way along, people sing hymns punctuated by the refrain: "Saint Stanislaus, our Patron, pray for us." The procession descends from Wawel, goes along Stradom and Krakowska Streets to Skałka, where the Holy Sacrifice of the Mass is celebrated, normally by a bishop invited for the occasion. After Mass the procession returns to the cathedral along the same route. The relics of the head of Saint Stanislaus, which were carried in a splendid reliquary during the procession, are placed on the altar. From the very beginning Poles were convinced of the saintliness of this bishop and made fervent efforts to have him canonized. The canonization took place at Assisi in the thirteenth century. Frescoes representing Saint Stanislaus have been preserved to this day in the Umbrian city.

Next to the reliquary of Saint Stanislaus is one of the greatest treasures of Wawel Cathedral—the tomb of Queen Saint Hedwig. Her relics were placed under the famous Wawel Crucifix in 1987 on the occasion of my third pilgrimage to my homeland. It was at the feet of this Crucifix that the twelve-year-old Hedwig made the decision to marry the Lithuanian prince Władysław Jagiełło. This decision of 1386 brought Lithuania into the family of Christian nations.

June 8, 1997, was a very emotional day for me. In the Błonia area of Kraków, during the canonization, I began my homily with the words: "You have waited a long time for this day, Hedwig—nearly six hundred years." A great variety of circumstances were responsible for this long delay. It is difficult to speak of them now. I had long cherished the wish that the Lady of Wawel might one day glory in the title of saint in the canonical, official sense, and that day my wish was granted. I thanked God that after so many centuries it was my privilege to fulfill this aspiration, which beat in the hearts of so many generations of Poles.

All these memories are somehow linked to the day of my consecration that, in a sense, was an historical event. The last episcopal ordination in Wawel Cathedral had taken place back in 1926. Then, Bishop Stanisław Rospond was consecrated. Now it was my turn.

The Day of the Ordination:
At the Heart of the Church

September twenty-eighth came. It was the memorial of Saint Wenceslaus, the day designated for my episcopal ordination. I constantly think of that great ceremony (in those days the Liturgy was even richer than it is today) and I remember every single person who took part.

There was a custom of offering symbolic gifts to the ordaining bishop, including a small barrel of wine and a loaf of bread. These were carried by my friends: Zbyszek Siłkowski, a schoolmate from high school, and Jurek Ciesielski, now Servant of God; next came Marian Wójtowicz and Zdzisław Heydel. Stanisław Rybicki was probably also there. The most active one was certainly Father Kazimierz Figlewicz. The day was cloudy, but later the sun came out. As if by some good omen—a ray of sunshine fell on the poor new bishop.

After the reading of the Gospel the choir sang: *"Veni Creator Spiritus, mentes tuorum visita: imple superna gratia, quae tu creasti pectora. . . ."* I listened intently to the singing of this hymn and once again, as during my priestly ordination, and maybe with even greater clarity, I became conscious that it was the Holy Spirit who effected this consecration. This was a source of comfort and consolation in the face of all the human fears associated with this great new responsibility. The thought filled my soul with deep trust: the Holy Spirit will enlighten me, strengthen me, comfort me, and teach me. . . . Did not Jesus make this promise to His Apostles?

In the Liturgy there follows a series of symbolic actions each with its own meaning. The ordaining bishop asks certain questions relating to faith and life. The last question is as follows: *"Are you resolved to pray for the people of God without ceasing, and to carry out the duties of one who has the fullness of the priesthood so as to afford no grounds for reproach?"* The candidate responds: *"I am, with the help of God."* Then the ordaining bishop adds: *"May God who has begun the good work in you bring it to fulfillment."* That thought of trust and peace returned: the Lord is beginning His work in you, fear not. Entrust your life to Him; He will act and fulfill His work (*Ps. 37; 36:5*).

At every ordination (whether of a deacon, priest, or bishop) the candidate prostrates himself. This is a sign of his total surrender to Christ, to the one who, in order to fulfill His priestly mission, *"emptied himself, taking the form of a slave . . . and being found in human form, he humbled himself, becoming obedient to death—even death on a cross" (Phil. 2:7–8).* A similar action occurs every Good Friday when the main celebrant of the Liturgy prostrates himself in silence. The Mass is not celebrated on that day of the Sacred Triduum. The Church gathers to meditate upon the Passion of Christ, beginning with His agony in the Garden, where He too prostrated Himself in prayer. The celebrant is forcibly reminded of Christ's words: *"Remain here and keep watch with me" (Matt. 26:38).*

I remember that moment when I was lying prostrate, and the assembled congregation was singing the Litany of the Saints. The ordaining bishop urged the congregation: *"My dear people, let us pray that Almighty God in his goodness will pour out the riches of his grace upon this servant of his, for the good of the Church."* Then began the singing of the litany:

> *Lord, have mercy. Christ, have mercy . . .*
> *Holy Mary, Mother of God,*
> *Saint Michael*
> *Holy Angels of God . . . pray for us*

I have a special devotion to my Guardian Angel. Probably like all children, during my childhood I would often pray: *"Angel of God, my guardian, be always with me . . . always stand ready to help me, guard my soul and my body. . . ."* My Guardian Angel knows what I am doing. My faith in him, in his protective presence, continues to grow deeper and deeper. Saint Michael, Saint Gabriel, Saint Raphael—these are the archangels I frequently invoke during prayer. I also recall that most beautiful treatise of Saint Thomas about angels—pure spirits.

> *Saint John the Baptist,*
> *Saint Joseph,*
> *Saints Peter and Paul,*
> *Saint Andrew,*
> *Saint Charles . . . pray for us!*

My ordination to the priesthood took place on the Feast of All Saints, which had always been an important feast for me. The goodness of God has allowed me to celebrate the anniversary of my priestly ordination on the day when the Church remembers all the saints in heaven. From on high they intercede for the Church that she may grow in communion through the action of the Holy Spirit, who inspires the practice of fraternal charity: "Exactly as Christian communion between men on their earthly pilgrimage brings us closer to Christ, so our community with the saints joins us to Christ, from whom as from its fountain and head issues all grace and the life of the People of God itself" (*Lumen Gentium*, 50).

After the litany the candidate rises and approaches the celebrant, who lays his hands on him. This gesture, according to a tradition that reaches back to the Apostles, signifies the handing on of the Holy Spirit. Then both co-consecrators also lay their hands on the head of the candidate. Next, the celebrant and the co-consecrators say the prayer of consecration. In this way the central moment of the rite of episcopal ordination is brought to completion. Here we should recall the words of the Dogmatic Constitution *Lumen Gentium*: "In order to fulfill such exalted functions, the apostles were endowed by Christ with a special outpouring of the Holy Spirit coming upon them (*cf. Acts 1:8; 2:4; John 20:22–23*), and, by the imposition of hands (*cf. 1 Tim. 4:14; 2 Tim. 1:6–7*), they passed on to their auxiliaries the gift of the Spirit, which is transmitted down to our day through episcopal consecration. . . . In fact, from tradition, which is expressed especially in the liturgical rites and in the customs of both the Eastern and Western Church, it is abundantly clear that by the imposition of hands and through the words of the consecration, the grace of the Holy Spirit is given, and a sacred character is impressed, in such wise that bishops, in a resplendent and visible manner, take the place of Christ himself, teacher, shepherd and priest, and act as his representatives" (n. 21).

The Ordaining Bishops

I must now speak of the principal celebrant—Archbishop Eugeniusz Baziak. I have already mentioned the complicated story of his life and episcopal ministry. His episcopal lineage is very important to me as it is through him that I am joined to the apostolic succession myself. He had been consecrated by Archbishop Bolesław Twardowski, who in turn was consecrated by Bishop Józef Bilczewski, whom I recently beatified in Lviv, in the Ukraine. Bilczewski was consecrated by Cardinal Jan Puzyna, archbishop of Kraków. Co-consecrators were Saint Józef Sebastian Pelczar, bishop of Przemyśl, and the Servant of God Andrzej Szeptycki, a Greek-Catholic archbishop. Does not all this impose some type of obligation? How could I not be mindful of this tradition of sanctity of these great pastors of the Church?

My co-consecrators were Bishop Franciszek Jop of Opole and Bishop Bolesław Kominek of Wrocław. I remember them with great respect and gratitude. Bishop Jop was a providential figure in Kraków during the Stalinist times. Archbishop Baziak was cut off from the diocese at that time, and Bishop Jop was designated the vicar capitular in Kraków. Thanks to him the Church in that city survived this period of trial without any great harm. Bishop Bolesław Kominek was also associated with Kraków. During the Stalinist period, when he was already bishop of Wrocław, the communist authorities forbade him to enter his diocese. He took up residence in Kraków as a mitred prelate. Only later was it possible for him to take canonical possession of his diocese, and in 1973 he was named a cardinal. These were both great churchmen who, in difficult times, gave an example of personal greatness and bore faithful witness to Christ and to the Gospel. How could I fail to be moved by this heroic spiritual heritage?

Gestures of the Ordination Liturgy

I recall other important liturgical gestures from my episcopal ordination, including the placing of the Book of the Gospels on the shoulders of the candidate while a special consecration prayer is sung. This union of sign and word is particularly eloquent. The initial impression directs the candidate's thought to the burden of a bishop's responsibility for the Gospel, the weight of Christ's invitation to carry it and proclaim it to the ends of the earth, and to bear witness to it through his own life. Looking more deeply into this eloquent sign, one realizes the truth that what is being accomplished is derived from the Gospel and is rooted there. The candidate who is being ordained can therefore draw strength and inspiration from this knowledge. It is in the light of the Good News about the Resurrection of Christ that the words of this prayer become intelligible and effective: *"Effunde super hunc Electum eam virtutem, quae a te est, Spiritum principalem, quem dedisti dilecto Filio tuo Iesu Christo, quem ipse donavit sanctis Apostolis. . . .* So now pour out upon this chosen one that power which is from you, the governing Spirit whom you gave to your beloved Son, Jesus Christ, the Spirit given by him to the holy apostles. . . . "[3]

There now follows the anointing with sacred Chrism. This gesture is deeply rooted in sacraments already received, beginning with Baptism and Confirmation. At a priestly ordination, the hands are anointed; at an episcopal ordination the head is anointed. This is another gesture that speaks of the imparting of the Holy Spirit, who enters within, takes possession of the candidate, and makes him His instrument. This anointing of the head signifies the call to new responsibilities: the bishop will have the task of guiding the Church, which will place great demands on him. This anointing by the Holy Spirit has the same source as the others: Jesus Christ—the Messiah.

The name Christ is a Greek translation of the Hebrew term *"mašiah"*—(messiah), which means "the anointed one." In Israel those who were chosen by Him to fulfill a particular mission were anointed in the name of God. This could be a prophetic, priestly, or kingly mission. The term "messiah," however, was applied above all to the one who would finally come to establish the Kingdom of God, in whom the promises of salvation were to be fulfilled. It was precisely he who was to be "anointed" with the Holy Spirit as prophet, priest, and king.

The designation *Christ—Anointed One* became the proper name of Jesus because the Divine mission that this name signifies was perfectly fulfilled in Him. The Gospels do not say that Jesus was ever anointed externally, like David or Aaron in the Old Testament, upon whose beard a precious ointment ran down (*Ps. 133; 132:2*). When we speak of Christ's "anointing," we mean the direct anointing by the Holy Spirit, signified and attested by Christ's perfect fulfillment of the mission entrusted to Him by His Father. Saint Irenaeus expressed this very beautifully: "For in the name of Christ is implied, He that anoints, He that is anointed and the unction itself with which He is anointed. And it is the Father who anoints, but the Son who is anointed by the Spirit, who is the unction."[4]

At Christ's birth the angels announced to the shepherds: *"Today in the city of David a Savior has been born for you who is Christ the Lord" (Luke 2:11).* "Christ" means the Anointed One. With Him is born both the universal, messianic, and salvific anointing, in which all the baptized participate, and also the special anointing that He, the Messiah, wished to share with bishops and priests chosen to exercise apostolic responsibility for

His Church. The sacred Oil of Chrism, a sign of the power of the Divine Spirit, flowed over our heads and integrated us into the messianic work of salvation. With this anointing we received in a specific manner the threefold mission: as prophet, priest, and king.

Sacred Chrism

I thank the Lord for *the first anointing with sacred Chrism* that I received in my hometown of Wadowice. It took place during my Baptism. We are all justified and clothed in Christ by this sacramental cleansing with water. We also receive the gift of the Holy Spirit for the first time. This anointing with Chrism is a sign of the outpouring of the Spirit, who gives new life in Christ and enables us to live in the righteousness of God. That first anointing is completed with the seal of the Holy Spirit received in the sacrament of Confirmation. The deep and direct bond between these sacraments is particularly evident in the Liturgy of Adult Baptism. The Eastern Churches, for their part, have also preserved this direct bond in infant baptism by conferring Baptism and Confirmation together.

These first two sacraments and the most holy mystery of the Eucharist are linked with the vocation to the priesthood and the episcopate by a bond so strong and deep that it constantly reveals new riches to our grateful hearts. We bishops have not only received these sacraments ourselves, but we are sent to baptize, to gather the Church around the Table of the Lord, and to strengthen the disciples of Christ with the seal of the Holy Spirit in the sacrament of Confirmation. A bishop, in the course of his ministry, has many opportunities to confer this sacrament. By anointing candidates with sacred Chrism, he imparts to them the gift of the Holy Spirit, who is the source of life in Christ.

In many places during ordinations, you can hear the faithful sing: *"Priestly people, royal nation, holy assembly, people of God, sing to your Lord!"* I like the rich content of this hymn.

> *We sing to You, beloved Son of the Father!*
> *We glorify You, eternal Wisdom, living Word of God.*
> *We sing to You, only Son of the Virgin Mary,*
> *We adore You, Christ, our Brother,*
> *You have come to save us.*
> *We sing to You, Messiah, welcomed by the poor,*

We adore You, O Christ, our King so humble and
  meek (. . .)
We, Your branches, sing to You, O life-giving Vine.

All vocations are born in Christ, and this is what is
expressed by every anointing with Chrism—from holy
Baptism to the anointing of the head of a bishop. This
is the source of the dignity common to all Christian
vocations, which, from this point of view, are all equal.
They differ according to the role that Christ assigns to
each individual within the community of the Church
and the responsibility attached to the role. Great care
must be taken so that *"nothing is wasted" (John 6:12)*: no
vocation should be wasted because all are valuable and
necessary. The Good Shepherd gave His life for the lives
of all *(John 10:11)*. This is precisely the responsibility of
a bishop: he should realize that it is his duty to ensure
that all who are chosen and called by Christ, even the
least, can discover and fulfill their vocation in the
Church. That is why a bishop, like Christ, calls, gathers,
and teaches around the Table of the Body and Blood of
Christ. At the same time, the bishop both leads and
serves. He must be faithful to the Church—and to each
of its members, even to the least whom Christ has
called and with whom He identifies *(Matt. 25:45)*. As a
sign of this fidelity the bishop receives a ring.

The Ring and the "Rationale"

The ring on the bishop's finger signifies that he is married to the Church. *"Accipe anulum, fidei signaculum*—Take this ring, the sign of your fidelity. In integrity of faith and purity of life, protect the holy Church, bride of Christ. *Esto fidelis usque ad mortem . . ."* These words are taken from the Book of Revelation—*"Be faithful until death, and I will give you the crown of life" (Rev. 2:10).*

This ring, a nuptial symbol, expresses the particular bond between the bishop and the Church. For me it is a daily call to fidelity. It is like a silent question that echoes in my conscience: Am I totally dedicated to my Bride—the Church? Am I sufficiently "for" the communities, families, young and old people, and also "for" those yet to be born?

My ring also reminds me of the need to be a strong link in the chain of succession that stretches back to the Apostles. And the strength of a chain is measured by its weakest link. I must be a strong link, strong with God's own strength: *"The Lord is my strength and my shield"* (Ps. 28; 27:7). *"Even though I walk through a dark valley, I fear no harm, for you are at my side; your rod and your staff give me courage"* (Ps. 23; 22:4).

The bishops of Kraków enjoy a special privilege, reserved, as far as I know, to just four dioceses in the world. They have the right to wear the so-called rationale. Outwardly it resembles the pallium. In Kraków it is kept in the treasury of Wawel Cathedral—a gift from Queen Hedwig. In itself this sign means nothing. It acquires significance only when the archbishop wears it. It then symbolizes his authority and his service: because he has authority, he must serve. In a sense, it is a symbol of the Passion of Christ and of all the martyrs. As I put it on, I often recalled the words of the elderly Apostle Paul to the still young bishop Timothy: *"So do not be ashamed of your testimony to our Lord, nor of me, a prisoner for His sake; but bear your share of hardship for the gospel with the strength that comes from God!"* (2 Tim. 1:8).

"Guard What Has Been Entrusted to You" (1 Tim. 6:20)

After the prayer of consecration, the ritual provides for the presentation of the Book of Gospels to the new bishop. This gesture indicates that the bishop is to accept and preach the Good News. He is a sign of the presence in the Church of Jesus, the teacher. Teaching is of the essence of a bishop's calling—he too must be a teacher.

We know how many outstanding bishops, from ancient times to the present, have fulfilled this mission in a most exemplary way. They cherished the prudent advice of the Apostle Paul as an admonition addressed personally to them: *"O Timothy, guard what has been entrusted to you. Avoid profane babbling and the absurdities of so-called knowledge" (1 Tim. 6:20).* They were good teachers because they built their entire spiritual life around the Word, listening to it and proclaiming it. In other words they were able to put aside unnecessary words and devote themselves wholeheartedly to the *"one thing necessary" (Luke 10:42).*

The bishop is to become the servant of the Word. Precisely as a teacher he sits on the cathedra—the chair eloquently situated in the church known for that reason as the "cathedral," from which he is to preach, proclaim, and explain the Word of God. Our times have placed new demands on bishops with regard to their teaching office, but have also offered them wonderful new resources to help them preach the Gospel. The ease of travel has enabled bishops to visit the various churches and communities in their own diocese more frequently. They have at their disposal radio, television, the Internet, the printed word. There are others who assist the bishop in proclaiming the Word of God: priests and deacons, catechists and teachers, professors of theology, and an ever-growing number of educated laypersons faithful to the Gospel.

But nothing can take the place of the bishop seated upon the cathedra or standing in the pulpit of his episcopal church, personally expounding the Word of God to those gathered around him. And he, like *"every scribe who has become a disciple of the kingdom of heaven, is like the head of a household who brings from his storeroom things old and new" (Matt. 13:52).* Here I wish to mention the archbishop emeritus of Milan, Cardinal Carlo Maria Martini, whose catechesis in the cathedral attracted crowds of listeners to whom he revealed the treasure of God's Word. This is only one of many examples that prove how hungry the people are for the Word of God. How important that this hunger be satisfied.

I have always been convinced that if I am to satisfy the people's hunger for the Word of God, I must follow the example of Mary and first listen to it myself *and ponder it in my heart (Luke 2:19)*. I have also come to realize that a bishop must be able to listen to the people to whom he preaches the Good News. Amid today's flood of words, images, and sounds, it is important that a bishop not be thrown off course. He must listen attentively to God and to those around him, convinced that we are all united in the one mystery of God's saving Word.

The Miter and Crosier

The call to become a bishop is certainly a great honor. This does not mean, however, that he is chosen for having distinguished himself among many others as an outstanding person and Christian. The honor comes from his mission to stand at the heart of the Church as the first in faith, first in love, first in fidelity, and first in service. If someone seeks in the episcopal office honor for its own sake, he will not be able to fulfill his episcopal mission well. The first and most important aspect of the honor due to a bishop lies in the responsibility associated with his ministry.

"A city set on a mountain cannot be hidden" (Matt. 5:14). The bishop is always on a mountain, always on a lampstand, visible to all. He must always be aware that what-

ever happens in his life takes on greater meaning in his community. *"And the eyes of all looked intently at him"* (*cf. Luke 4:20*). Just as a father shapes the faith of his children primarily by his example of prayer and religious fervor, so also a bishop inspires his faithful by his behavior. That is why the author of the First Letter of Peter begs that bishops be *"a living example to the flock"* (*1 Pet. 5:3*).

In this context, the investiture with the miter during the ordination liturgy is an especially eloquent sign. The newly ordained bishop receives the miter as a reminder of his commitment to let the "light of holiness will shine in him" and to prove worthy "to receive the unfading crown of glory" when Christ, the "Supreme Shepherd," will appear.[5]

A bishop is called to personal holiness in a particular way so that the holiness of the Church community entrusted to his care may increase and deepen. It is his responsibility to promote the "universal call to holiness" of which the fifth chapter of the Dogmatic Constitution *Lumen Gentium* speaks. As I wrote at the conclusion of the Great Jubilee, this vocation constitutes *"an intrinsic and essential aspect"* of ecclesiology (*Novo millennio ineunte*, 30). The people of God, "brought into unity from the unity of the Father, the Son and the Holy Spirit," is a people that belongs to the One who is *"thrice holy"* (*cf. Isa. 6:3*). "To profess the Church as holy," I wrote, "means to point to her as the *Bride of Christ*, for whom He gave Himself precisely in order to make her holy" (*Novo millennio ineunte,* 30). The gift of holiness becomes the goal. We must constantly remind ourselves that the entire life of a Christian must be directed toward this goal: *"This is the will of God, your holiness" (1 Thess. 4:3).*

At the beginning of the 1970s, referring to the Dogmatic Constitution *Lumen Gentium,* I wrote: "The history of salvation is the history of the whole People of God, which also pervades the lives of individuals and takes a new specific form in each. The essential meaning of holiness is that it is always personal, and that each and every man is called to it. All members of the people of God are called, but each is called in a unique and unrepeatable manner."[6]

The personal holiness of every individual gives added beauty to the face of the Church, the Bride of Christ. This enables our contemporary world to accept her message more easily.

The presentation of the crosier comes next in the ordination liturgy. It is a sign of the authority that enables the bishop to fulfill his duty to care for his flock. Like other signs, it too speaks of the bishop's solicitude for the holiness of the People of God. A shepherd must watch and protect, must lead every sheep *"into green pastures" (Ps. 23; 22:2),* where the sheep will discover that holiness is not "some kind of extraordinary existence, possible only for a few 'uncommon heroes' of holiness. The ways of holiness are many, according to the vocation of each individual" (*Novo millennio ineunte*, 31). What a great potential of grace lies dormant in the vast numbers of the baptized! I constantly pray that the Holy Spirit may set ablaze the hearts of bishops with His fire, so that we may become teachers of holiness, able to attract the faithful by our example.

I recall the moving farewell of Saint Paul to the elders of the Church in Ephesus: *"Keep watch over yourselves and over the whole flock of which the Holy Spirit has appointed you overseers, in which you tend the Church of God that He acquired with His own blood"* (Acts 20:28). The command of Christ urges every shepherd: *"Go . . . and make disciples of all nations"* (Matt. 28:19). Go . . . never stop! How well we know the Divine Master's expectation: *"I chose you and appointed you to go and bear fruit that will last"* (John 15:16).

The crosier with the Crucifix that I presently use is a replica of the crosier of Paul VI. I see in it a symbol of three duties: pastoral care, leadership, and responsibility. It is not a sign of authority in the usual sense of the word, nor is it a sign of precedence or supremacy over others: it is a sign of service. As such, it is a sign of the care I must show for the needs of the sheep: *"that they might have life and have it more abundantly!"* (John 10:10). A bishop must guide and lead. The faithful will listen to him and love him to the degree that he imitates Christ, the Good Shepherd, who *"did not come to be served but to serve and to give his life as a ransom for many"*

(Matt. 20:28). To serve! How I treasure those words! A priesthood of service—what an astounding title . . .

Sometimes you hear people defending the idea that a bishop's authority should be understood as precedence: they say the sheep are to follow behind the shepherd, not the shepherd behind the sheep. One can agree with this, but only in the sense that the shepherd leads by *giving his life for his sheep*; he should be first in sacrifice and in dedication. *"The Good Shepherd who laid down his life for his sheep is risen from the dead. For the sake of his flock he was willing to endure death."⁷* The bishop's precedence takes the form of a generous love for the faithful and for the Church, in imitation of Saint Paul: *"Now I rejoice in my sufferings for your sake, and in my flesh I am completing what is lacking in the afflictions of Christ for the sake of his body, which is the Church"* (Col. 1:24).

Another responsibility that certainly forms part of a pastor's role is admonition. I think that in this regard I did too little. There is always a problem in achieving a balance between authority and service. Maybe I should have been more assertive. I think this is partly a matter of my temperament. Yet it could also be related to the will of Christ, who asked His Apostles not to dominate but to serve. Obviously a bishop has authority, but much depends on the way he exercises it. If a bishop stresses his authority too much, then the people think all he can do is issue commands. On the other hand, if he adopts an attitude of service, the faithful spontaneously tend to listen to him and willingly submit to his authority. So a certain balance is needed. If a bishop says: "I'm in charge here" or "I'm only here to serve," then something is missing: He must serve by ruling and rule by serving. We have an eloquent model of this dual approach in Christ Himself: He served unceasingly, but in the spirit of serving God He was also able to expel the money changers from the temple when this was needed.

I do think, though, that despite my reluctance to rebuke others, I made all the necessary decisions. As the metropolitan of Kraków I tried very hard to make those decisions in a collegial spirit, that is to say I consulted my auxiliary bishops and other coworkers. Every week we met for curial sessions during which all matters were discussed in the light of the greater good of the archdiocese. I used to put two questions to my coworkers: *"Which truth of faith sheds light on this problem?"* And then: *"Whom should we approach for assistance?"* Finding a religious motivation for our action and the right person for a particular task was a good beginning, offering hope that our pastoral initiatives would bear fruit.

The presentation of the crosier concludes the rite of ordination. Then begins the Mass, which the new bishop concelebrates with the ordaining bishops. This is all so rich in meaning, in reflections, and in personal thanksgiving that it cannot be adequately expressed nor can anything more be added.

Pilgrimage to the Shrine of Our Lady

After Mass I went directly from Wawel Cathedral to the seminary where the reception was held for invited guests, but that same evening I went to Częstochowa with a group of my closest friends. There, on the following morning, I celebrated Mass in the chapel of the miraculous image of Our Lady.

Częstochowa is a special place for Poles. In a sense it can be identified with Poland and its history, especially the history of the struggle for independence. Here stands the national shrine called Jasna Góra—the Bright Mountain. *Clarus Mons*: This name refers to the light that dispels darkness, and it took on a special meaning for Poles during the dark times of war, partition, and occupation. Everyone knew that the source of this light

51

of hope was the presence of Our Lady in her miraculous image. It was so, perhaps for the first time, during the terrible Swedish invasion known in history as "the deluge." At that time the shrine, significantly, became a fortress that the attackers could not conquer. The nation interpreted this sign as a promise of victory. Faith in Our Lady's protection gave the Poles the strength to conquer the invader. From that moment the Shrine of the Bright Mountain became in some sense a bastion of faith, spirit, and culture and all that constitutes national identity. This was especially true during the long years of the partitions and the loss of national independence. Pope Pius XII alluded to this during World War II when he said: "Poland has not perished nor will it perish because Poland believes, Poland prays, Poland has the Bright Mountain." And thanks be to God, those words proved true.

Later there came another dark period in our history—the communist regime. Party authorities were aware of what Jasna Góra meant to the Poles, likewise the miraculous icon, and the Marian devotion long associated with it. So when, on the initiative of the Polish episcopate, and especially Cardinal Stefan Wyszyński, a national pilgrimage with the Black Madonna set off from Częstochowa in order to visit every parish and community in Poland, the communist authorities did all in their power to stop it. When the icon was "arrested" by the police, the pilgrimage continued with the empty frame, and the message became even more eloquent. The frame with no picture was a silent sign of the lack of religious freedom in Poland. The nation knew it had a right to regain religious freedom and prayed fervently for it. This pilgrimage lasted for almost twenty-five years, and engendered among the Poles an extraordinary strengthening of faith, hope, and love.

All Polish Catholics make the pilgrimage to Częstochowa. I used to go on pilgrimage there from my youngest days. In 1936 there was a great pilgrimage of students from all over Poland, concluding with a solemn vow before the icon. Since that time, the pilgrimage has been repeated every year.

During the Nazi occupation I made the pilgrimage as a student of Polish philology in the department of philosophy at the Jagiellonian University. I remember it particularly because, to uphold the tradition, we went to Częstochowa as delegates: Tadeusz Ulewicz, I, and a third person. Jasna Góra was surrounded by Hitler's troops. The eremitical Pauline Fathers were our hosts and they knew we belonged to a delegation. This was obviously a matter of great secrecy. But we had the satisfaction of upholding the tradition, against all the odds. Later I often visited the shrine with various pilgrimages, especially the one from Wadowice.

Every year the bishops made their retreat at Jasna Góra, usually at the beginning of September. The first time I took part I was simply a bishop-elect, and it was Archbishop Baziak who took me with him. I remember that the preacher on that occasion was Father Jan Zieja, an outstanding priest. The first place, naturally, was taken by the Primate, Cardinal Stefan Wyszyński, a truly providential man for the times we were living through.

These pilgrimages to Jasna Góra may have given birth to my desire to begin my pilgrim journeys as Pope by visiting a Marian shrine. This desire led me to make my first apostolic journey to Mexico, at the feet of Our Lady of Guadalupe. The love that the Mexicans and the people of Latin America in general have for Our Lady of Guadalupe—a love expressed spontaneously and emotionally, but intensely and profoundly—is very similar to the Polish Marian devotion that shaped my own spirituality. They affectionately call Mary *La Virgen Morenita*, which can be freely translated as "the Black Madonna." There is a popular Mexican song about the love of a young man for a young lady, which the people address to Our Lady. Those melodious words linger in my ears:

Conocí a una linda Morenita . . . y la quise mucho.
Por las tardes iba yo enamorado y cariñoso a verla.
Al contemplar sus ojos, mi pasión crecía.
Ay Morena, morenita mía, no te olvidaré.
Hay un Amor muy grande que existe entre los dos,
   entre los dos . . .

I met a beautiful dark-skinned woman and came
    to like her very much.
Evenings—full of love and affection—I would
    walk to see her.
When I looked into her eyes, my love grew.
O dark-skinned woman, my dark-skinned woman,
    I will not forget you.
There is a great love between us, between us . . .

I visited the shrine at Guadalupe during my first apostolic pilgrimage in January 1979. The decision to travel there was made in response to an invitation to take part in a meeting of the Conference of Bishops of Latin America at Puebla de los Angeles. To some degree, this pilgrimage inspired and shaped all the succeeding years of my pontificate.

First I stopped in Santo Domingo, after which I went on to Mexico. Something extraordinarily moving happened while we were making our way to our quarters for the night: As we crossed streets heaving with crowds, we could almost touch with our hands, so to speak, the devotion of these countless people. When we finally reached our destination, where we were to spend the night, the people just kept on singing—and it was already midnight. Then Father Stanisław Dziwisz realized he would have to go out and silence the crowd, explaining to them that the Pope had to get some sleep. Only then did they quiet down.

I remember that I looked upon that journey to

Mexico as a kind of "permit," which would make it possible for me to go on pilgrimage to Poland. I thought that the communists in Poland wouldn't be able to refuse me permission to return to my country after I had been received in a country with so secular a constitution as Mexico had at the time. I wanted to go to Poland, and this desire came to fruition in June of that same year.

Guadalupe, the largest shrine in all of North America, is for that continent what Częstochowa is for Poland. Certainly they belong to two quite different worlds: Guadalupe to a Latin-American world; Częstochowa to a Slavic world, to Eastern Europe. This became clear during World Youth Day in 1991, when for the first time young people from beyond the eastern borders of Poland gathered in Częstochowa: Ukrainians, Latvians, Belorussians, Russians. . . . Every region of Eastern Europe was represented.

But to return to Guadalupe, in 2002 I was privileged to celebrate the canonization of Juan Diego in this shrine. It was a wonderful opportunity to offer thanks to God. Juan Diego, having embraced Christianity without surrendering his indigenous identity, discovered the profound truth about the new humanity, in which all are called to be children of God in Christ. *"I bless you, Father, Lord of heaven and earth, for although you have hidden these things from the wise and the learned you have revealed them to mere children. . . ." (Matt. 11:25).* And in this mystery, Mary had a very particular role.

THE MINISTRY
OF A BISHOP

"Fulfill your ministry" (2 Tim. 4:5)

The Duties of a Bishop

Upon my return to Kraków from my first pilgrimage to Częstochowa as a bishop, I began work in the archdiocesan curia, and was immediately named vicar general. I can honestly say that I soon made friends with all those working for the Kraków curia: Father Stefan Marszowski, Father Mieczysław Satora, Father Mikołaj Kuczkowski, and Father Bohdan Niemczewski, a mitred prelate. The latter, as dean of the Chapter of Canons, was later to be a strong advocate of my appointment as archbishop, despite the strongly aristocratic tradition there—archbishops of Kraków were usually chosen from among the aristocracy. And so it was a great surprise when after such a long line I, from the "proletariat," was named Archbishop of Kraków.

But this happened some years later, in 1964. I will return to this in due course.

I felt very much at ease in the curia and I recall the years in Kraków with deep gratitude and joy. Priests began coming to me with a great variety of problems. I worked with real enthusiasm. The visitation of parishes began in the spring.

Gradually I became accustomed to my new role in the Church. Episcopal ordination brought new responsibilities. They had been expressed in a brief, synthetic form during the liturgy of ordination. As I said earlier, the rite of episcopal ordination at the time of my own ordination in 1958 had already begun to change, while its essence remained unaltered. By ancient custom, established by the Fathers of the Church, the new bishop is asked in the presence of the people whether he promises to preserve the faith in its integrity and to fulfill the ministry entrusted to him. At present the questions are as follows:

Are you resolved by the grace of the Holy Spirit to discharge to the end of your life the office the Apostles entrusted to us, which we now pass on to you by the laying on of hands?

Are you resolved to be faithful and constant in proclaiming the Gospel of Christ?

Are you resolved to maintain the deposit of faith, entire and incorrupt, as handed down by the Apostles and professed by the Church everywhere and at all times?

Are you resolved to build up the Church as the Body of Christ and to remain united to it within the order of bishops under the authority of the successor of the Apostle Peter?

Are you resolved to be faithful in your obedience to the successor of the Apostle Peter?

Are you resolved as a devoted father to sustain the people of God and to guide them in the way of salvation in cooperation with the priests and deacons who share your ministry?

Are you resolved to show kindness and compassion in the name of the Lord to the poor and to strangers and to all who are in need?

Are you resolved as a good shepherd to seek out the sheep who stray and to gather them into the fold of the Lord?

Are you resolved to pray for the people of God without ceasing, and to carry out the duties of one who has the fullness of the priesthood so as to afford no grounds for reproach?[28]

These words are certainly deeply etched into the heart of every bishop. They echo the questions that Jesus put to Peter on the shore of the Sea of Galilee: *"'Simon, son of John, do you love me more than these?' He said to him, 'Yes, Lord, you know that I love you.' He said to him, 'Feed my lambs.' He then said to him a second time, 'Simon, son of John, do you love me?' He said to him, 'Yes, Lord, you know that I love you.' He said to him, 'Tend my sheep.' He said to him the third time, 'Simon, son of John, do you love me?' Peter was distressed that he had said to him a third time, 'Do you love me?' and he said to him, 'Lord, you know everything; you know that I love you.' Jesus said to him, 'Feed my sheep!'" (John 21:15–17).* Not "your" sheep but "my" sheep! It was He who created man. It was He who saved him. It was He who redeemed everyone, every single person, at the price of His blood!

The Shepherd

Christian tradition has adopted the biblical image of the shepherd in three forms: as the one who carries the lost sheep on his shoulders, as the one who leads his flocks to green pastures, and as the one who gathers his sheep with his staff and protects them from danger.

In all three images there is a recurring theme: *The shepherd is for the sheep, not the sheep for the shepherd.* He is bound so closely to them, if he is a real shepherd, that he is ready *to lay down his life for the sheep (John 10:11).* Every year during the twenty-fourth and twenty-fifth week of Ordinary Time, the *Liturgy of the Hours* presents Saint Augustine's long *Sermon "On the Shepherds."* [9] With reference to the Book of the Prophet Ezekiel, the bishop of Hippo strongly rebukes evil shepherds, who are concerned not for the sheep but only for themselves. "Let us see how the word of God, that flatters no one, addresses the shepherds who are feeding themselves, not the sheep. *'You take the milk, you clothe yourselves with the wool, you slaughter the fatlings; but you do not feed my sheep. The weak you have not strengthened, the sick you have not healed, the crippled you have not bound up, the strayed you have not brought back, the lost you have not sought; any strong one you have killed; and my sheep are scattered because there is no shepherd.'"*[10] Saint Augustine does, however, arrive at a very positive conclusion: "Good shepherds are not lacking, but they are in the one . . . all good shepherds are in the one, all are one reality. Let them feed the sheep—it is Christ who feeds them . . . in them is his voice, his love."[11]

Saint Gregory the Great has offered us further inspiring reflections on the subject of pastoral ministry: "We see around us a world full of priests, but it is very rare to find a laborer in God's harvest, because we are not doing the work demanded by our priesthood, although we accepted this office. . . . We give up the ministry of preaching, and, to our discredit, as I see it, we are called bishops but enjoy this honour in name only and not in practice. For the people entrusted to our care are abandoning God and we remain silent."[12] This annual reminder, which the Liturgy puts before us, invokes our sense of responsibility toward the Church.

"I Know My Sheep" (John 10:14)

The good shepherd knows his sheep and they know him"
(John 10:14). A bishop should try to ensure that as many
as possible of those who, together with him, make up
the local Church can come to know him personally. He
for his part will seek to be close to them, to know about
their lives—what gives joy to their hearts and what sad-
dens them. Such mutual acquaintance cannot be built
through occasional meetings: It comes from a genuine
interest in what is happening in their lives regardless of
age, social status, or nationality, whether they are close
at hand or far away.[13] It is difficult to formulate a sys-
tematic theory on how to relate to people, yet I was
greatly helped in this by the study of personalism
during the years I devoted to philosophy. Every human

being is an individual person and therefore I cannot program a priori a certain type of relationship that could be applied to everyone, but I must, so to speak, learn it anew in every case. Jerzy Liebert's poetry expresses this effectively:

> I study you, my friend,
> Slowly I study you, slowly.
> This difficult task, its gain,
> Brings joy to my heart and pain.[14]

It is very important for a bishop to have a rapport with his people and to know how to relate to them well. In my own case, significantly, I never felt that I was meeting an excessive number of people. Nonetheless, I was always concerned to safeguard the personal quality of each relationship. Every person is a chapter to himself. I always acted with this conviction, but I realize that it is something you can't learn. It is simply there, because it comes from within.

Interest in others begins with the bishop's prayer life: his conversations with Christ, who entrusts "His own" to him. Prayer prepares him for encounter with others. In such meetings, if we are truly open, we can come to know and understand one another, even when there is little time. I simply pray for everyone every day. As soon as I meet people, I pray for them, and this helps me in all my relationships. It's difficult for me to tell how others perceive this. You would have to ask them. Yet I always follow this principle: I welcome everyone as a person sent to me and entrusted to me by Christ.

I don't like the word "crowd," which seems too anonymous; I prefer the word "multitude," in Greek *"plēthos" (cf. Mark 3:7; Luke 6:17; Acts 2:6, 14:1, and elsewhere)*. Christ walked along the streets of Palestine and often great multitudes of people followed Him; the same was true of the Apostles. Naturally, my own office causes me to meet many people, sometimes great multitudes. That's how it was in Manila, where there were millions of young people. Yet in a case like that it would have been wrong to speak of an anonymous crowd. It was a community animated by a single ideal, which made it easy to establish a relationship with them. It's rather like that everywhere I go.

In Manila I beheld all of Asia. What a multitude of Christians! And how many millions of people on this continent still do not know Christ! I place great hope in the dynamic Church in the Philippines and in Korea. Asia: that is the mission we all share for the third millennium.

The Administration of Sacraments

The greatest treasure, the greatest riches at a bishop's disposal, are the sacraments, which he administers with the help of the priests he has ordained. Christ entrusted this treasure into the hands of the Apostles and their successors through His testament, according to the deepest theological meaning of that word as well as its simplest everyday usage. Christ, *"knowing that the hour had come to pass from this world to the Father" (John 13:1),* "then gave Himself as food to His marvelling Apostles" (hymn *"Pange Lingua"*), bidding them repeat the rite of the Last Supper "in memory of him": to break the bread and to offer the cup of wine—sacramental signs of His Body "given up" and His Blood "poured out."

After His death and resurrection, He conferred

upon them the power to forgive sins and administer the other sacraments, beginning with Baptism. The Apostles handed on this treasure to their successors. Together with preaching the word, the administration of the sacraments is a bishop's primary duty, to which all his other responsibilities are subordinate. His whole life and activity must be directed toward this goal.

We know that we need help to accomplish this. *"Lord, grant also to us such fellow workers, for we are weak and our need is greater."*[15] That is why we select and prepare worthy candidates and ordain them priests and deacons. With us they undertake the duty of preaching the word and administering the sacraments.

Such considerations should help shed light upon our daily duties and priorities. This pertains not only to celebrating the Eucharist and administering the sacrament of Confirmation, but also to baptizing children and those adults who have been prepared by our local Church to become disciples of Christ. Nor should we underestimate the importance of personally hearing confessions and visiting the sick to administer the sacrament of Anointing, instituted specifically for the sick. Another important duty for a bishop, which he shares with his pastors, is solicitude for the sanctity of marriage; when it is possible, he should celebrate marriages personally.

Priests, as coworkers of the bishop, naturally assume most of these duties. However, the personal involvement of the diocesan pastor in the administration of sacraments is a good example for all the people of God entrusted to him, both laity and priests. It is the most eloquent sign of his bond with Christ, present and active in each of these sacramental mysteries. Christ Himself wishes us to be instruments of the work of salvation that He accomplishes through the sacraments of the Church. These effective signs of grace reveal to the human soul the face of Christ, merciful Redeemer and Good Shepherd. A bishop who personally administers the sacraments clearly demonstrates to all the faithful that he is a sign of Christ, who is always present and active in His Church.

Pastoral Visits

I have already mentioned that I used to work regularly at the curia, but I particularly enjoyed pastoral visitations. I liked them very much because they put me in direct contact with people. I had a strong sense that I was "forming" them. Priests and laity, young people and old, the healthy and sick, parents with their children and their problems—all came to me with whatever was on their mind. That was life.

I remember well my first pastoral visitation to Mucharz, south of Wadowice. The parish had an elderly pastor, an excellent priest, a monsignor. His name was Józef Motyka. He knew this was my first pastoral visitation and he was moved by this. He told me this could be his last. He felt he should be my guide. The visitation embraced the entire deanery and lasted the months of May and June. After the summer vacation, I visited my home deanery, Wadowice.

Visitations took place in the spring and in the fall. I did not manage to visit all of the parishes (there were more than three hundred of them); in spite of the fact that I was a bishop in Kraków for twenty years, I didn't get to them all. I remember that the last parish I visited in the archdiocese of Kraków was Saint Joseph in Złote Łany, a new residential area of Bielsko-Biała. I spent the night at the Divine Providence parish, where Father Józef Sanak was pastor. On my return from this visitation, I offered Mass for the repose of the soul of Pope John Paul I and then went to Warsaw to participate in the meetings of the Episcopal Conference. After this I set off for Rome . . . not knowing that I would have to remain there.

My pastoral visitations were rather long; maybe that's why I didn't manage to visit all the parishes. I worked out my own model for carrying out this pastoral responsibility. There was, in fact, a traditional model with which I began when I visited Mucharz. The old monsignor whom I met there was a valuable tutor. Later, after acquiring some experience, I introduced certain changes. I was not happy with an unduly juridical approach; I wanted the visitations to be more pastoral.

I worked out a particular pattern. The visitation

always began with a welcome ceremony in which various persons and groups took part: adults, children, and young people. Then they took me to the church where I gave an address in order to establish a rapport with the people. The next day I first heard confessions for an hour or two, depending on the circumstances.

Then I celebrated Mass and visited homes, especially the homes of sick people. Unfortunately, the communists would not allow me to visit hospitals. The sick were also brought to church for a special ceremony. The Servant of God Hanna Chrzanowska took care of this aspect of the visitation throughout the diocese. I have always been very conscious of the fundamental importance of what the suffering contribute to the life of the Church. I remember that at the beginning the sick intimidated me. I needed a lot of courage to stand before a sick person and enter, so to speak, into his physical and spiritual pain, not to betray discomfort, and to show at least a little loving compassion. Only later did I begin to grasp the profound meaning of the mystery of human suffering. In the weakness of the sick, I saw emerging ever more clearly a new strength—the strength of mercy. In a sense, the sick provoke mercy. Through their prayers and sacrifices, they not only ask for mercy but create a "space for mercy," or better, open up spaces for mercy. By their illness and suffering they call forth acts of mercy and create the possibility for accomplishing them. I used to entrust the needs of the Church to the prayers of the sick, and the results were always positive. During a visitation I would also administer the sacraments: confirming young people and celebrating marriages.

I would meet separately with different groups, such as teachers, parish workers, and young people. There was also a special gathering in church for all married couples. Mass would be celebrated, concluding with an individual blessing for each couple. The homily would naturally be dedicated to the subject of marriage. I always felt moved when I encountered large families and expectant mothers. I wanted to express my respect for motherhood and fatherhood. From the beginning of my priesthood, I have always had a special pastoral concern for married couples and families. As a chaplain to university students, I regularly organized marriage preparation courses, and later, as a bishop, I promoted the pastoral care of families. These experiences, these meetings with engaged couples, married couples, and families, gave birth to my poetic drama *The Jeweler's Shop*, my book *Love and Responsibility*, and, more recently, my *Letter to Families*.

There were also separate meetings with the clergy. I wanted to give an opportunity to each of them to confide in me, to share the joys and concerns of their particular ministry. I greatly valued these meetings; they enabled me to learn from the treasury of wisdom accumulated over many years of apostolic labor.

The way pastoral visitations were conducted varied according to the circumstances in a given parish. Their situations were, in fact, very diverse. For example, the parish visitation to the Basilica of the Assumption in Kraków lasted two months, as there are so many churches and chapels there. The visitation to Nowa Huta was totally different. There was no church there, even though there were tens of thousands of inhabitants. There was just a small chapel adjoining the old school. It must be remembered that in those post-Stalin times, the government waged war with religion. It would not allow the construction of new churches in a socialist city such as Nowa Huta was intended to be.

The Battle for a Church

Here at Nowa Huta there was a hard battle to build a church. The neighborhood was home to many thousands of inhabitants, mainly workers from all over Poland employed in the large metallurgical industry. According to the authorities, Nowa Huta was to be a perfect model of a socialist city, that is to say, with no link of any kind to the Church. Yet it was impossible to forget that the people who went there in search of work had no wish to abandon their Catholic roots.

The struggle began in the large residential area of Bieńczyce. At the beginning, the communist authorities yielded to pressure, and gave permission to build a church and designated the land for it. Immediately the local people erected a cross there. This permission, however, granted during the time of Archbishop Baziak, was later withdrawn, and the authorities decreed the removal of the cross. The faithful vehemently opposed this. There followed a confrontation with the police in which some people were injured. The mayor asked us to calm the people. This was one of the first incidents in a long battle for freedom and dignity by the population whose destiny had brought them to this new district of Kraków.

In the end the battle was won, but at the cost of a lengthy war of nerves. I conducted discussions with the authorities, mainly with the head of the provincial Office for Religious Affairs. He was truly polite in conversation but stubborn and unrelenting in making decisions, and this betrayed his malice and bias.

Father Józef Gorzelany, the pastor, undertook the task of building the church and brought it to a successful conclusion. He made a wise pastoral suggestion to his parishioners. He asked each of them to bring a stone that would be used for the foundations and the walls, so that everyone felt personally involved in the construction of the new church.

We experienced the same kind of situation in Mistrzejowice. This episode revolved around the heroic Father Józef Kurzeja, who came to me on his own initiative and requested that he be assigned to minister in that district. There was a small structure there in which he wanted to begin catechism classes in the hope that slowly he would be able to build a new parish. It came to pass, but the fight to build a church in Mistrzejowice cost Father Kurzeja his life. Oppressed by the communist authorities, he died of a heart attack at the age of thirty-nine.

Father Kurzeja was helped in his fight to build a church in Mistrzejowice by Father Mikołaj Kuczkowski, who, like myself, was a native of Wadowice. I remember him from his days as an attorney when he was engaged to Nastka, a beautiful girl who was the president of the Catholic Youth Association. When she died, he decided to become a priest. He entered the seminary in 1939 and began his philosophical and theological studies, which he completed in 1945. I was very close to him, and he was also fond of me. He wanted, as we say, "to make someone of me." After my ordination as a bishop, he personally took charge of my move to the episcopal residence on 3 Franciszkańska Street. I repeatedly had occasion to learn of his great affection for Father Józef Kurzeja, the first pastor in Mistrzejowice and a simple, good man (one of his sisters became a Sister of the Sacred Heart). As I mentioned, Father Kuczkowski was of great help to him in his pastoral activity, and when Father Kurzeja died, he resigned from the office of chancellor of the curia to take his place in the parish at Mistrzejowice. Now both lie buried in the crypt of the church they built.

Much could be said about them. For me, they were

an eloquent example of priestly fraternity that, as a bishop, I observed and encouraged with admiration: *"A faithful friend is a sturdy shelter; he who finds one finds a treasure" (Sirach 6:14)*. True friendship is born of Christ: *"I have called you friends . . ." (John 15:15)*.

Bishop Ignacy Tokarczuk, of the neighboring diocese of Przemyśl, made significant progress in the matter of building churches in the People's Republic of Poland. He built them illegally, at the cost of many sacrifices and much harsh treatment from the local communist authorities. In his case, though, the situation was more favorable, because the communities in his diocese were predominantly rural villages, without the same difficulties that urban communities had. In the country, not only were the people more interested in religion, but they were less subject to the control of the police.

I remember with deep gratitude and admiration all the pastors who were building churches in Poland during that time and all those throughout the world who have built churches. I have always tried to support them. One way of expressing my support was through my celebrations of Christmas Midnight Mass at Nowa Huta, under the open sky, regardless of the freezing temperatures. I had already done this in Bieńczyce, and I was to do the same in Mistrzejowice and among the hills of Krzesľawice. It gave added force to our negotiations with the authorities: The people had a right, we would remind them, to participate in public expressions of their faith in more humane conditions.

I mention all this because our experiences at that time show what a great variety of pastoral responsibilities a bishop can have. These events speak of the living experience of a shepherd in caring for the flock entrusted to him. I have personally experienced the truth of the Gospel saying about the sheep following their shepherd: *"They will not follow a stranger because they recognize the voice of their shepherd. He also has other sheep that do not belong to his fold. These too he must lead"* (cf. John 10:4–5; 16).

INTELLECTUAL AND PASTORAL RESPONSIBILITIES

" . . . Full of goodness, filled with all knowledge"
(Rom. 15:14)

The Faculty of Theology in the Context of Other University Faculties

As a bishop in Kraków, I felt obliged to defend the faculty of theology at the Jagiellonian University. I considered it my duty. The communist authorities maintained that this faculty had been transferred to Warsaw. Their pretext for this was that in 1953 the Academy of Catholic Theology had been established in the capital, under state control. The battle was won thanks to the fact that an autonomous Pontifical faculty of theology was later established, followed by the Pontifical academy of theology.

Sustaining me throughout this struggle was the conviction that scholarship, in its many different manifestations, is a priceless treasure for a nation. Obviously, in my exchanges with the communist authorities, it was the study of theology that I was arguing for, since its survival was under threat. Yet I never forgot other areas of scholarship, including those which might seem far removed from theology.

With regard to other disciplines, most of my contacts were with physicists. In the course of our many encounters, we would speak, for example, of the most recent discoveries in cosmology. This was a fascinating study, which confirmed for me Saint Paul's dictum that certain knowledge of God can also be reached through knowledge of the created world (*cf. Rom. 1:20–23*). Those meetings in Kraków still continue today, from time to time, in Rome or in Castel Gandolfo, thanks to the efforts of Professor Jerzy Janik.

I have always been concerned with providing appropriate pastoral care for scientists. Their chaplain in Kraków for a time was Professor Father Stanisław Nagy, whom I recently made a cardinal, partly as a way of showing my appreciation for Polish science.

The Bishop and the World of Culture

It is well known that not all bishops are particularly interested in a dialogue with scholars. Many of them give greater priority to their pastoral responsibilites, understood in the broadest sense, than to their rapport with men of learning. In my view, however, members of the clergy, priests and bishops, do well to take the trouble to establish personal contacts with the academic world and its leading figures. A bishop, in particular, should be concerned not only with his own Catholic academic institutions, but should also maintain close links with the whole university world: reading, meeting others, discussing, informing himself about their activities. Obviously, he himself is not called to be a scholar but a pastor. Yet as a pastor, he cannot fail to take an interest in this part of his flock, since it is his task to remind scholars of their duty to serve the truth and thus to promote the common good.

In Kraków I also tried to maintain a good rapport with the philosophers: Roman Ingarden, Władysław Stróżewski, and Andrzej Półtawski; and with the priest-philosophers: Kazimierz Kłósak, Józef Tischner, and Józef Życiński. My personal philosophical outlook moves, so to speak, between two poles: Aristotelian Thomism and phenomenology. I was particularly interested in Edith Stein, an extraordinary figure, for her life story as well as her philosophy. Born into a Jewish family in Wrocław, she discovered Christ, was baptized and entered the Carmelite convent, spent some time in the Netherlands, but was deported from there to Auschwitz by the Nazis. She died in a gas chamber and her mortal remains were burned in a crematorium. She had studied with Husserl and had been a colleague of the Polish philosopher Ingarden. I had the joy of beatifying her in Cologne and then canonizing her in Rome. I also proclaimed Edith Stein, Sister Teresa Benedicta of the Cross, as a copatron of Europe, together with Saint Bridget of Sweden and Saint Catherine of Siena: three women alongside the three male patrons: Cyril, Methodius, and Benedict.

I was interested in her philosophy. I read her writings, especially *Endliches und Ewiges Sein (Finite and Eternal Being)*, but what fascinated me most was her extraordinary life and her tragic destiny, intertwined with that of millions of other defenseless victims of our era. A disciple of Edmund Husserl, an impassioned seeker after truth, an enclosed nun, a victim of Hitler's regime: hers is a truly unique human story.

Books and Study

The responsibilities that weigh on a bishop's shoulders are many. I have discovered this for myself and I know how hard it is to find time for everything. Yet this experience has also taught me the great need a bishop has for recollection and study. He has to have a profound theological formation, constantly updated, and a wide-ranging interest in thought and culture. These are treasures that all thinking people share. For this reason I would like to say something about the importance of reading in my life as a bishop.

This has always been a dilemma for me: What am I to read? I have always tried to choose what was most essential. So much has been published and not everything is valuable and useful. It is important to know how to choose and to consult others about what is worth reading.

From my earliest childhood I have loved books. It was my father who introduced me to reading. He would sit beside me and read to me, for example, Sienkiewicz and other Polish writers. After my mother died, the two of us remained alone. He continued to encourage me to explore good literature and he never stood in the way of my interest in the theater. But for the outbreak of war and the radical change that it brought, maybe the prospects opening up for me through academic study would have absorbed me completely. When I told Mieczysław Kotlarczyk of my decision to become a priest, he said, "What are you doing? Do you want to waste your talent?" Only Cardinal Sapieha had no doubts.

As a university student I read many different authors. First I turned to literature, especially plays. I read Shakespeare, Molière, the Polish poets Norwid, Wyspiański, and, of course, Aleksander Fredro. My greatest love, however, was acting, appearing on stage, and I often wondered which characters I would like to play. Kotlarczyk and I would amuse ourselves by assigning roles to each other and wondering who could best play a particular part. These are things of the past. Later someone said to me, "You have talent . . . you'd have been a great actor if you'd stayed in the theater."

The Liturgy is also a kind of acted *mysterium*, played

out on stage. I remember the deep emotion I felt when, as a fifteen-year-old boy, I was invited by Father Figlewicz to the Sacred Triduum at Wawel Cathedral, and I was present for the Tenebrae services, brought forward to the Wednesday afternoon of Holy Week. It was a profound spiritual experience for me, and to this day I find the Triduum extremely moving.

Then came the time for philosophical and theological literature. As a clandestine seminarian, I was given the manual on metaphysics by Professor Kazimierz Wais of Lwów. Father Kazimierz Kłósak said, "Study this! When you've learnt it, you'll take the exam." For a few months I immersed myself in the text. I took the exam and I passed. This was a turning point in my life— a whole new world opened up before me. I began to engage with theological books. Later, during my studies in Rome, I took a deep interest in the *Summa Theologiae* of Saint Thomas Aquinas.

So there were two stages to my intellectual journey: In the first I moved from literature to metaphysics, while the second led me from metaphysics to phenomenology. This was the grounding for my own scholarly work. The first stage coincided initially with the Nazi occupation, when I was working in the Solvay factory and secretly studying theology at the seminary. I remember that when I presented myself to the rector, Father Jan Piwowarczyk, he said, "I will accept you, but not even your mother is to know that you are studying here." That was the situation. But I was able to make progress all the same. Later on, Professor Father Ignacy Różycki helped me greatly by taking me into his home and providing me with a base for my studies.

Much later, Father Różycki suggested the topic for my habilitation thesis on Max Scheler's book *Der Formalismus in der Ethik und materiale Wertethik,* which I translated into Polish as I was writing my thesis. This was another turning point. I defended the thesis in November 1953. My readers were Father Aleksander Usowicz, Stefan Żwieżawski, and theologian Father Władysław Wicher. This was the last habilitation granted by the faculty of theology at the Jagiellonian University before its suppression by the communist authorities. The faculty, as I mentioned earlier, was transferred to the Academy of Catholic Theology in Warsaw, but I was able to begin teaching at the Catholic University in Lublin in the fall of 1954, thanks to the assistance of Professor Żwieżawski; he became a good friend and has remained so to this day.

I was fond of Father Różycki, whom I called Ignac, and he was equally fond of me. It was he who encouraged me to take the exam for my habilitation, and he acted as a kind of supervisor. For some years we lived together and took our meals together. Our cook was Maria Gromek. I remember my room perfectly. It was in the residence of the Wawel Cathedral Chapter at 19 Kanonicza Street, and for six years it was my home.

After that I moved to number twenty-one, and finally, through the good offices of the chancellor, Father Mikołaj Kuczkowski, I moved into the episcopal palace at 3 Franciszkańska Street.

In my reading and in my studies I always tried to achieve a harmony between faith, reason, and the heart. These are not separate areas, but are profoundly interconnected, each giving life to the other. This coming together of faith, reason, and the heart is strongly influenced by our sense of wonder at the miracle of a human person—at man's likeness to the Triune God, at the immensely profound bond between love and truth, at the mystery of mutual self-giving and the life that it generates, at our reflections on the succession of human generations.

Children and Young People

I want to dedicate a special part of these reflections to children and young people. Aside from my meetings with them during parish visitations, I always devoted great attention to students, particularly university students, because the city of Kraków is traditionally a lively center of academic study. There were many opportunities for us to meet: from lectures and debates to days of recollection and retreats. Of course, I also kept in close contact with the priests who were assigned to pastoral ministry in this area.

As the communists suppressed all Catholic youth associations, a way had to be found to remedy the situation. The Servant of God, Father Franciszek Blachnicki, came upon the scene and initiated the so-called

Oasis Movement. I became closely involved with this movement and tried to support it in every way possible. I defended it before the communist authorities, I supported it financially, and, obviously, I took part in its activities. During the summer vacation I would often visit the so-called oases, which were camps organized for the young people belonging to the movement. I would preach to them, speak with them, climb mountains with them, and sing with them around the fire. I frequently celebrated Mass for them in the open air. This all added up to a really intensive pastoral program.

During my pilgrimage to Kraków in 2002, the young people of the Oasis Movement sang this song:

> Lord, you have come to the seashore,
> Neither searching for the rich nor the wise,
> Desiring only that I should follow.
> O Lord, with your eyes set upon me,
> Gently smiling, you have spoken my name,
> All I longed for I have found by the water,
> At your side, I will seek other shores.

I told them that this oasis song led me, in a way, from my homeland to Rome. Its profound meaning was a support to me when I had to respond to the decision reached by the conclave. And throughout my pontificate, I have never forgotten the message of this song. What is more, I am constantly reminded of it not only in Poland but in other countries of the world. Whenever I hear it, I remember those meetings I had with young people. I greatly value this wonderful experience. I brought it with me to Rome. Here too, I looked for ways to put it to good use, taking as many opportunities as I could to meet young people. In a sense, the World Youth Days could be seen as a fruit of that experience.

Another youth movement that I encountered as a bishop was the so-called Sacrosong. It was a kind of festival of religious music and song, accompanied by prayer and reflection. These gatherings took place all over Poland and attracted large numbers of young people. I often took part myself, helping with the organization and supporting them financially. I have good memories of these gatherings. I have always enjoyed singing. To tell the truth, I used to sing whenever the occasion arose, but I enjoyed singing with young people most of all. The texts were varied, depending on the occasion: Around the fire we sang folk songs and scout songs. For national feast days, the anniversary of the outbreak of war, or the Warsaw Uprising, we would sing military and patriotic songs. My favorites were *"Red Poppies on Monte Cassino," "The First Brigade,"* and songs about the Polish insurrection and the resistance in general.

The rhythm of the liturgical year is a further factor determining the choice of music. At Christmastime in

Poland there are many songs devoted to the Lord's Nativity, while those heard during the approach to Easter are concerned with the Passion. These old Polish hymns cover the whole range of Christian theology. They constitute a treasury of living tradition that speaks to the hearts of every generation and shapes their faith. During the months of May and October, in addition to Marian hymns, we sing the litanies and the Little Office of the Blessed Virgin Mary. What poetic riches are contained in these popular hymns that are still sung today! As a bishop I tried to cultivate this tradition, which young people were particularly keen to maintain. I believe that we all benefited greatly from this treasury of simple and deep faith that our forefathers expressed in these hymns.

On May 18, 2003, I canonized Mother Urszula Ledóchowska, a great educator. She was born in Austria, but at the end of the nineteenth century the whole family moved to Lipnica Murowana in the diocese of Tarnów. She also lived in Kraków for a few years. Her sister Maria Teresa, known as Mother of Africa, has been beatified, and her brother, Włodzimierz, was the Superior General of the Jesuits. The example of these brothers and sisters illustrates how the desire for holiness can develop in a remarkable way if it finds favorable surroundings in a good family. So much depends on life in the home! Saints beget and raise saints!

When I remember educators like Mother Urszula, I

instinctively think of children. During my pastoral visitations in Poland, as well as those that I make here in Rome, I have always tried and I still try to find time to meet young children. I have never stopped encouraging priests to devote a generous amount of time to them in the confessional. It is very important to form the consciences of children and young people. I have recently spoken of the importance of receiving Holy Communion worthily (*Ecclesia de Eucharistia*, 37). It is at the confession preceding First Communion that the proper disposition can be prepared. I daresay each of us can recall the first confession that we made as a child.

My predecessor Saint Pius X gave a touching testimony to his pastoral love for children by the changes he introduced regarding the reception of First Holy Communion. Not only did he lower the age for approaching the Eucharistic Table (I was able to take advantage of this in May 1929), but he also introduced the possibility of receiving Communion before the age of seven, if the child demonstrates sufficient understanding. This pastoral decision to bring forward the reception of Holy Communion is most commendable. It has yielded rich fruits of holiness in children and in the apostolate among the young, in addition to a flowering of priestly vocations.

I have always been convinced that without prayer, we can never succeed in bringing children up well. As a bishop I encouraged families and parish communities to develop in young children a desire to encounter God in private prayer. In this spirit I recently wrote: "To pray the rosary *for children*, and even more, *with children*, . . . is a spiritual aid which should not be underestimated."[16]

The pastoral care of children must obviously be continued as they enter adolescence. Frequent confession and spiritual direction help young people to discern their vocation in life and protect them from losing their way as they enter adulthood. I remember Pope Paul VI saying to me during a private audience in November 1964: "My dear brother, today we must be very attentive toward our young students. The main focus of our pastoral care as bishops should be on priests, workers, and students." I believe that these words came from personal experience. When he worked in the Secretariat of State, Giovanni Battista Montini was involved for many years in the pastoral care of university students in his capacity as the General Assistant of the Italian Catholic University Federation, or FUCI (Federazione Universitaria Cattolica Italiana).

Catechesis

We have been entrusted with the mission to *"go and make disciples of all nations" (cf. Matt. 28:19–20)*. In today's social context, we do this best through catechesis, which should be based both upon reflection on the Gospels and on our understanding of the things of this world. We need to understand the experiences of the people around us and the language they use to communicate. This is an important task for the Church. Pastors must be generous in sowing the seed, even though others will gather the harvest of their labors. *"I tell you, look up and see the fields ripe for the harvest. The reaper is already receiving his payment and gathering crops for eternal life so that the sower and the reaper can rejoice together. For here the saying is verified that 'One sows and* another reaps.' I sent you to reap that for which you did not labor; others have done the work, and you are sharing the fruits of their work" (John 4:35–38).

We fully realize that catechesis cannot rely solely on abstract concepts. Obviously they are necessary because, when we speak of supernatural realities, we cannot avoid the use of philosophical concepts. Catechesis, however, gives priority to the human person and to personal encounter through signs and symbols of faith. Catechesis is always love and responsibility, a responsibility born of love for those whom we meet on our journey.

The new *Catechism of the Catholic Church*, which was presented to me for approval in 1992, came to birth because of a desire to make the language of faith more accessible to people today. The image of the Good Shepherd, used as the "logo" on the cover of every edition of the *Catechism*, is highly significant. It is taken from a third-century Christian tombstone, found in the catacombs of Domitilla. The figure "suggests certain characteristic aspects of the Catechism: Christ, the Good Shepherd who leads and protects his faithful (the lamb) by his authority (the staff), draws them by the melodious symphony of the truth (the panpipes) and makes them lie down in the shade of the 'tree of life,' his redeeming Cross which opens paradise."[17] It is an image that speaks of the Shepherd's concern for *every sheep*— a concern filled with the patience needed to reach every *individual* in a truly personal way. It also includes the *gift of tongues*, that is the *gift of speaking in a language understood by all the faithful*. We should pray to the Holy Spirit for this gift.

Sometimes a bishop can more easily establish a rapport with adults by blessing their children and giving them some of his time. This is worth more than a long discourse on respect for the weak and defenseless. Today much imagination is needed if we are to learn how to speak about the faith and about life's most important questions. It requires people who know how to love and how to think, because the imagination lives on love and on thought, as well as nourishing our thinking and enkindling our love.

Caritas

One of a pastor's duties is concern for the least, as that word is understood in the Gospels. In the Acts of the Apostles and the Letters of Saint Paul, we read about collections organized by the Apostles to provide for the needs of the poor. I should like to mention here the example of Saint Nicholas, bishop of Myra in Asia Minor during the fourth century. At that time, the Christians of the East and the West were not yet divided, and both traditions are represented in the devotion to this saint. In fact, he is equally venerated in both East and West. His person, though shrouded in many legends, continues to exert a certain fascination, especially on account of his goodness. Children in particular turn to him with deep trust.

How many of our problems can be resolved when we begin with confident prayer! As children we all waited for Saint Nicholas to bring us presents. The communists wanted to deprive him of his sanctity, so they invented Grandfather Frost. Unfortunately, in the West, Nicholas has now become popular in the context of consumerism. Nowadays people seem to have forgotten that his goodness and generosity were, first and foremost, the measure of his holiness. He distinguished himself as a bishop by his great concern for the poor and needy. I remember that as a child I had a personal devotion to him. Naturally, like every other child, I looked forward to the gifts he would bring me on December sixth. But this expectation had a religious dimension too. Like my peers, I felt a certain veneration toward this saint who unselfishly lavished gifts upon the people, thereby demonstrating his loving concern for them.

In the Church today, the part once played by Saint Nicholas in providing for the needs of the least has been assumed by the institute known as Caritas. In Poland, the communist authorities suppressed this organization, whose protector after the war had been Cardinal Sapieha. As his successor I tried to revive it and support its activities. Monsignor Ferdynand Machay, archpriest of the Basilica of the Assumption in Kraków, helped me greatly in this. Through him I came to know the Servant of God, Hanna Chrzanowska, whom I mentioned earlier, daughter of the distinguished professor Ignacy Chrzanowski, who was arrested at the beginning of the war. I remember him clearly, even though I never had the opportunity to get to know him well. Thanks to the efforts of Hanna Chrzanowska, the apostolate among the sick emerged and started to take shape in the archdiocese. There were many different activities including retreats for the sick in Trzebinia, particularly significant occasions involving many people, among them numerous young volunteers.

In my Apostolic Letter written for the beginning of the new millennium, I reminded everyone of the need for even greater resourcefulness in this area. "Now is the time for a new 'creativity' in charity" (*Novo millennio ineunte,* 50). How could I fail to mention, in this context, that great Missionary of Charity, Mother Teresa of Calcutta?

In the days immediately following my election to the See of Peter, I met this great little missionary sister, who from then on would often visit me to tell me where and when she had succeeded in opening new houses to provide a home for the poorest. After the fall of the communist party in Albania, I was able to visit that country. Mother Teresa was also there. Albania, of course, was her native land. I met her on many other occasions, and every time I was able to witness new signs of her passionate commitment to care for the poorest of the poor. Mother Teresa died in Calcutta, warmly remembered for her wonderful work, which her great multitude of spiritual daughters would continue. During her lifetime many people already regarded her as a saint, and when she died, her sanctity was universally recognized. I thank God that I was privileged to beatify her on October 19, 2003, around the time of the twenty-fifth anniversary of my pontificate. I said then, "The witness of Mother Teresa's life reminds us all that the Church's evangelizing mission is achieved through charity and is nourished through prayer and attentive listening to the Word of God. This missionary style is eloquently expressed by the image of Blessed Teresa clasping the hand of a child while fingering her rosary beads with her other hand. Contemplation and action, evangelization and respect for the human person: Mother Teresa proclaims the Gospel through her life of total dedication to the poor and total dedication to prayer."

This is the mystery of evangelization through love of neighbor springing from love for God. This is the essence of that *caritas*, which should inspire everything a bishop says and does.

THE FATHERHOOD
OF A BISHOP

*"I kneel before the Father, from whom every family
in heaven and on earth takes its name"
(Eph. 3:14–15)*

Cooperation with the Laity

The laity can accomplish their proper vocation in the world and attain holiness not only through their active involvement in helping the poor and needy, but also by imbuing society with a Christian spirit as they carry out their professional duties and offer an example of Christian family life. Here I am thinking not only of leaders in public life but also of the many people who can transform their daily life into prayer, placing Christ at the center of their activity. He will draw them all to Himself and satisfy their *hunger and thirst for righteousness (cf. Matt. 5:6)*.

Isn't this the lesson we can learn from the final part of the parable of the Good Samaritan (*Luke 10:34–35*)? After bandaging the wounds of the victim, the

Samaritan brought him to the innkeeper and asked him to look after him. Without the innkeeper, what could he have done? It was really the innkeeper, behind the scenes, who did most of the work. We can all do as he did—carrying out our duties in a spirit of service. Directly or indirectly, every occupation provides opportunities to help the needy. This is especially true in the case of doctors, teachers, or businessmen, provided always that they keep their eyes open to the needs of others. But it is also true of employees, workers or laborers who can find plenty of opportunities to be of service to their neighbors—even if they have serious problems of their own. By faithfully carrying out our professional duties, we are already expressing our love for individuals and for society.

The bishop, for his part, is called not only to become personally involved in Christian charitable works of this kind, but also to encourage the emergence and development of further initiatives planned and directed by others in his diocese. Yet he should always be vigilant that the work is accomplished in charity and in fidelity to Christ, *"pioneer and perfecter of faith" (cf. Heb. 12:2)*. We must go in search of the right people, but we should also be ready to allow all people of good will to take their place in the home that is the Church.

As a bishop I supported many different lay activities. They included, for example, the Apostolate to Families, the Kler-med seminars for clerics and medical students, the Institute for the Family. Before the war, Catholic Action was very active in Poland—it was divided into four groups: men, women, male youth, and female youth—and is now experiencing a revival. I was also chairman of the Commission for the Lay Apostolate in the Polish episcopate. I supported the Catholic publication, *Tygodnik Powszechny,* and did all I could to encourage the group who were involved with it. This was extremely necessary at that time. Editors, scholars, doctors, and artists all came to see me. As this was during the time of the communist dictatorship, they sometimes had to come secretly. We also organized conferences: the bishop's home was nearly always occupied, full of life. And the Sisters of the Sacred Heart had to feed everybody . . .

I also supported various new initiatives in which I could sense the inspiration of the Holy Spirit. Only when I came to Rome did I encounter the Neocatechumenate. The same was true of Opus Dei, which I established as a personal prelature in 1982. These two ecclesial movements call forth a great commitment from the laity. They both originated in Spain, a country that so often throughout history has been the source of providential inspirations for spiritual renewal. In October 2002 I had the joy of canonizing Josemaría Escrivá de Balaguer, the founder of Opus Dei, a zealous priest, and an apostle to the laity in modern times.

During the years of my ministry in Kraków, I always felt spiritually close to the Focolare movement. I admired their intense apostolic activity, directed toward helping the Church to become ever more "the home and school of communion." Since I was called to the See of Peter, I have often received Chiara Lubich, together with representatives of the various branches of the Focolare movement. Another movement to have emerged from the vitality of the Italian Church is Comunione e Liberazione, promoted by Monsignor Luigi Giussani.

There are many more lay initiatives that I have come to know in recent years. In France, Jean Vanier's L'Arche and Foi et lumière come to mind. There are others, but it's impossible to name them all. For now, I will just say that I support them, and remember them in my prayers. I have great hopes for them, and above all I wish that through them Christ's call might be heard and answered: *"You go into my vineyard too" (Matt. 20:4)*. I was thinking of them when I wrote this passage in the Apostolic Exhortation *Christifideles laici*: "The call is a concern not only of Pastors, clergy, and men and women religious. The call is addressed to everyone: lay people as well are personally called by the Lord, from whom they receive a mission on behalf of the Church and the world."

Cooperation with Religious Orders

I have always had good relations with religious orders and worked well with them. Kraków probably has a greater concentration of religious orders, both male and female, than any other diocese in Poland. Many were founded there and many others took refuge there, including the Felician Sisters, who came from the territories of the former Kingdom of Poland. My thoughts turn to Blessed Honorat Koźmiński, who founded several female religious orders without a habit—the fruit of his zealous work in the confessional. In this regard he was a genius. The foundress of the Felician Sisters, Blessed Mother Angela Truszkowska, now buried in their church in Kraków, worked under his direction. I should emphasize that the largest religious families in

Kraków are the medieval ones, such as the Franciscans and the Dominicans, as well as the sixteenth-century orders like the Jesuits and the Capuchins. These orders enjoy a reputation for good confessors, among clergy as well as laity. (The priests in Kraków often choose Capuchins as their confessors.) At the time of the partitions of Poland, many orders found themselves in the archdiocese because, not having permission to operate in the then Kingdom of Poland, they crossed the border into the Republic of Kraków, where they could enjoy relative freedom. The clearest example of my good relations with the religious orders was the episcopal nomination of Albin Małysiak of the Congregation of the Mission (Vincentian). He had been a zealous pastor in Kraków—in Nowa Wieś—and it was I who put him forward as a candidate, together with Stanisław Smoleński, and I consecrated them both.

The religious orders never caused me any problems, and my relations with all of them were good. They were a great help to me in my mission as a bishop. My thoughts also turn to the great reserves of spiritual energy found in the contemplative orders. There are two Carmelite convents in Kraków, one on Kopernika Street and the other on Łobzowska Street. There are also the Poor Clares, the Dominican Sisters, the Visitation Sisters, and the Benedictine Sisters in Staniątki. These are great centers of prayer and penance, as well as catechesis. I remember saying once to the enclosed nuns: "May this grille join you to the world and not separate you from it. Embrace the whole world with your mantle of prayer!" I am convinced that these dear sisters all over the world are always conscious that they exist for the world and never cease to serve the universal Church through their self-giving, silence, and fervent prayer.

Every bishop can find great support in them. I experienced this many times when, faced with a difficult problem, I would ask certain contemplative orders for the support of their prayers. I felt the power of their intercession and I would thank those sisters gathered in their Upper Rooms of prayer for helping me to overcome situations that, humanly speaking, seemed hopeless.

The Ursuline Sisters ran a boarding school in Kraków and Mother Angela Kurpisz always invited me to meet with the students during their retreat. I often visited the Gray Ursulines in Jaszczurówka (Zakopane) and took advantage of their hospitality each year. A tradition arose that every New Year's Eve at midnight I would celebrate Mass with the Franciscans in Kraków and in the morning I would go to stay with the Ursulines in Zakopane for some skiing (there was usually enough snow at that time). I normally stayed with them until January sixth, when I would leave during the afternoon so as to be back in time to celebrate the six o'clock Mass at the Cathedral in Kraków. Afterward, we would gather in Wawel and sing Christmas carols. I remember that on one occasion I had gone skiing, probably with Father Józef Rozwadowski (who later became bishop of Łódź), and we got lost somewhere around the Chochołowska valley. So we had to rush like madmen, as the saying goes, in order to get back in time.

For my days of recollection I would often go to the Albertine Sisters at Czerwony Prądnik, where I felt very much at home, and also to Rząska just outside Kraków. I was also on good terms with the Little Sisters of Charles de Foucauld and sometimes worked with them.

As I mentioned earlier, I used to spend a great deal of time at the Benedictine Abbey of Tyniec, where I made my retreats. I knew Father Piotr Rostworowski well and often made my confession to him. I also knew Father Augustyn Jankowski, a biblical scholar and a teaching colleague of mine. He always sends me his latest books. For my days of recollection I would go to Tyniec or to the Camaldolese Fathers in Bielany. As a young priest I led a retreat in Bielany for university students from Saint Florian's parish. I remember that on one occasion I went down to the church late at night and, to my great surprise, found the students praying there. I then discovered that they were planning to take turns to pray there throughout the night.

Religious orders serve both the Church and the bishop. How can one fail to admire their witness of faith based on the vows of poverty, chastity, and obedience, and their manner of life inspired by the Rule drawn up by their founder! Thanks to such fidelity, the various religious families can maintain their original charism and draw fruit from it in successive generations. Nor can one forget the example of fraternal charity at the heart of every religious community. It's only human that problems can arise from time to time, but a solution can always be found, provided that the bishop is able to listen attentively to the community, respecting its legitimate autonomy, and provided that the community, for its part, duly acknowledges the bishop's ultimate responsibility for pastoral oversight of the whole diocese.

The Presbyterate

There were always a good many vocations in the Archdiocese of Kraków, and in some years the number was exceptionally high. After October 1956, for example, the applications to the seminary increased significantly, and the same thing happened ten years later, during the millennium of Polish Christianity. This seems to be the rule: after a great event there are more vocations. They issue from the ordinary daily life of the People of God. Cardinal Sapieha used to say that the seminary is the *pupilla oculi*, the pupil of a bishop's eye, just as the noviatate is for the religious superior. This is easy to understand: Vocations are the future of a diocese, and of a religious order, and ultimately the future of the Church. I personally devoted particular attention to seminaries. Every day, now, I pray for the Roman Seminary and for all the seminaries in Rome, throughout Italy, in Poland, and all over the world.

I pray especially for the seminary in Kraków, where I received my own formation, and in this way I wish to pay my debt of gratitude. When I was the bishop of Kraków, I showed a special interest in following vocations. At the end of June, I would ask how many applicants there were for the following year. Later, once they had been admitted, I would meet each one individually, ask about his family, and together we would try to discern his vocation. I would invite seminarians for morning Mass in my chapel and then offer them breakfast. This was an excellent way to get to know them. I joined them for dinner on Christmas Eve at the seminary or I invited the seminarians to join me in Franciszkańska Street. They didn't return to their families for the big feasts, so I wanted somehow to compensate them for this sacrifice. All these things I was able to do when I was in Kraków. In Rome it is more difficult because there are so many seminaries. Nonetheless, I have personally visited all of them, and when I've had the opportunity, I have invited the rectors to the Vatican.

No bishop should fail to challenge young people with the great ideal of the priesthood. A young heart can understand the reckless love that is needed for total self-giving. There is no greater love than Love with a capital "L." On May 3, 2003, in Madrid, during my last pilgrimage to Spain, I confided in the young people: "I was ordained a priest at the age of twenty-six. Fifty-six years have passed since then. Looking back, and remembering those years of my life, I can assure you that it is worth dedicating yourselves to the cause of Christ, and for love of Him, dedicating yourselves to the service of others. It is worth giving your lives for the Gospel and for your brothers and sisters!" The young people understood the message and echoed my words by chanting over and over again: *"It's worth it! It's worth it!"*

Concern for vocations is also manifested in the care taken over the selection of candidates for the priesthood. The bishop entrusts many aspects of this process to his collaborators, the seminary formation team, but he himself bears the final responsibility for the formation of priests. During the rite of ordination, it is the bishop who definitively chooses and calls the candidates in Christ's name when he says: *"We rely on the help of the Lord God and our Savior Jesus Christ, and we choose these men, our brothers, for priesthood in the presbyteral order."*[18] It is a great responsibility. Saint Paul warns Timothy: *"Do not lay hands too readily on anyone" (cf. 1 Tim. 5:22).* It is not a question of severity, but rather a sense of responsibility for the immensely precious gift that has been placed in our hands. It is for the sake of the gift and the mystery of salvation that such stringent demands are made in connection with the priesthood.

Here I would like to mention Saint Józef Sebastian Pelczar (1842–1924), bishop of the diocese of Przemyśl, whom I had the privilege of canonizing on my eighty-third birthday, together with Mother Urszula Ledóchówska, of whom I spoke earlier. This holy bishop was widely known in Poland for his writings, among which I would like to single out his book *Meditations on the Life of a Priest: Priestly Asceticism*. The book was published in Kraków while he was still a professor at the Jagiellonian University. (A new edition of the book appeared a few months ago.) It was the fruit of his rich interior life and it had a profound influence on whole generations of Polish priests, especially during my time. My own priesthood too was in some way formed by this ascetical work.

Tarnów and nearby Przemyśl are among the dioceses with the greatest number of vocations in the world. Archbishop Jerzy Ablewicz of Tarnów was a good friend of mine. He came from Przemyśl, so he was heir to the spiritual heritage of Saint Józef Pelczar. They were very demanding pastors, firstly with themselves and then with their priests and seminarians. I believe that this was the key to the large number of vocations in their dioceses. Challenges and high ideals are attractive to the young.

The unity of the presbyterate has always been close to my heart. In order to facilitate my contact with the priests, I set up a presbyteral council in 1968, just after the Council, as a forum in which to discuss programs for the priests' pastoral activity. At regular intervals throughout the year, meetings were organized in different regions of the archdiocese that would address specific issues raised by the priests themselves.

By his manner of life, a bishop demonstrates that the Christ as "Model" lives on and still speaks to us today. One could say that a diocese reflects the manner of life of its bishop. His virtues—chastity, a spirit of poverty and prayer, simplicity, sensitivity of conscience—will, as it were, be written into the hearts of his priests. They, in their turn, will convey these values to the faithful entrusted to their care, and in this way young people can be led to a make a generous response to Christ's call.

In considering our priests, we must not overlook those who have left the active ministry. The bishop cannot forget them. They too have a right to his paternal concern. Their stories sometimes indicate failures in priestly formation, which has to include courageous fraternal correction when it is called for. A priest, for his part, has to be ready to accept such correction. Christ said to his disciples: *"If your brother sins against you, go and tell him his fault between you and him alone. If he listens to you, you have won over your brother"* (Matt. 18:15).

The Bishop's Residence

My opportunities to meet the people came not only during pastoral visitations and other public events. The door of my residence at 3 Franciszkańska Street was always open to everyone. A bishop is a shepherd; so he should be with the people, for the people, and at the service of the people. Everyone had direct access to me at all times. All were welcome to my home.

All kinds of meetings and scholarly gatherings took place there, including the *Studium for the Family*. There was a special family consulting room. Those were times when the authorities looked upon any large gathering of laity as antigovernment activity. The bishop's residence became a place of refuge. I invited all sorts of people: scholars, philosophers, humanists. I also held regular meetings with priests, and the parlor was frequently used for lectures, for example by the Institute for the Family and by Kler-med. You might say that the residence was throbbing with life.

The episcopal residence in Kraków is filled with memories associated with my great predecessor, remembered by generations of priests in Kraków as an incomparable example of the paternal quality called for in a bishop. Cardinal Adam Stefan Sapieha was popularly known as the Indomitable Prince throughout the war and the occupation. He undoubtedly holds a special place in the story of my own vocation. It was he who encouraged me from the very beginning, as I have recounted in my book *Gift and Mystery*.

Prince Cardinal Sapieha was a Polish aristocrat in the true sense of the word. He was born in Krasiczyn near Przemyśl. I once made a special trip there just to see the castle in which he was born. He was ordained a priest for the diocese of Lviv. He worked in the Vatican during the pontificate of Pius X, acting as assistant secret chamberlain. He did a great deal of good for the Polish cause at that time. In 1912 he was named a bishop and was ordained by Saint Pius X himself for the see of Kraków. He took possession of the see that same year, just before the First World War, in other words. After the outbreak of hostilities, he established the Bishop's Committee for War Victims, commonly known as the Prince-Bishop's Committee, in

Kraków. In due course the Committee expanded its activities to include the whole country. The archbishop was extraordinarily active during the war years and for this he was greatly respected all over Poland. He became a cardinal only after the Second World War. Since the days of Cardinal Oleśnicki, a number of archbishops of Kraków had been cardinals before him, including Dunajewski and Puzyna, but it was Sapieha who earned the title of "Indomitable Prince."

It's true: Sapieha was a fine role model for me, principally because he was a shepherd. Even before the Second World War broke out, he had told the Pope that he wanted to retire from the see of Kraków, but Pius XII did not agree to this. He said to him: "War is coming; you will be needed." He died as the Cardinal of Kraków at the age of eighty-two.

During the funeral homily, the Primate of Poland, Cardinal Wyszyński, asked some very significant questions: "And so, dear brother priests of Kraków, as we, your guests and your friends, behold with what a rich wreath of emotions you surround this coffin that hides the mortal remains of that tiny figure that could overcome you neither by his height nor by his physical strength—I want to ask you for my own benefit, to increase that pastoral wisdom necessary for a bishop, what was it in him that you loved so much? What captured your hearts? What was it that you saw in him? Why did you surrender yourselves, like the whole of

Poland, to this soul? Here, we can truly speak of the love of a diocesan presbyterate for its archbishop."[19]

His funeral in July 1951 was an unprecedented event in the Stalinist era. A huge procession made its way from Franciszkańska Street to Wawel Cathedral—tightly packed rows of priests, sisters, and laity walked together. As they walked, the communist authorities did not dare disturb the procession. They felt helpless. That could have been the reason why, after instituting proceedings against the Kraków Curia, they did the same to Cardinal Sapieha once he was dead. The communists didn't dare touch him while he was alive. The cardinal knew it was a possibility, especially after the arrest of Cardinal Mindszenty. But they didn't have the courage.

I went to seminary as one of his students, receiving first the tonsure and then priestly ordination. I had great trust in him, and I can say that I loved him just as other priests loved him. It has often been said in books that Sapieha was in some way preparing me—maybe it's true. This too is a bishop's responsibility: to prepare possible successors.

Maybe the priests respected him because he was a prince, but they loved him first and foremost because he was a father who cared about people. This is what counts most of all: a bishop must be a father. True, no one can attain perfect fatherhood, because this is fully realized only in God the Father. But we can somehow participate in this fatherhood of God. I wrote about this truth in my meditation on the mystery of fatherhood, entitled *Radiation of Fatherhood*: "I will say more: I have decided to eliminate from my vocabulary the word 'my.' How can I use that word when I know that everything is Yours? Even if it isn't You who give birth every time a human person is born, the one giving birth belongs to You. I myself am more 'Yours' than 'mine.' So I have learned that I may not say 'mine' of that which is Yours. I may not say, think or feel it. I must free myself, empty myself of this—I must possess nothing, I must not wish to possess anything (here 'my' means 'my own')."[20]

Fatherhood Modeled on the Example of Saint Joseph

There is no doubt that the episcopate is an office, but a bishop must resist with all his strength any tendency to become a mere official. He must never forget that he is a father. As I said earlier, Cardinal Sapieha was so greatly loved because he was a father to his priests. When I wonder who could serve as a help and a model for all those called to fatherhood—whether in the family or in the priesthood, or even more so in the episcopate—it is Saint Joseph who comes to mind.

For me, devotion to Saint Joseph is another thing I would associate with my life in Kraków. The Bernardine Sisters on Poselska Street, near the episcopal palace, have a church dedicated to Saint Joseph, where they have perpetual adoration of the Blessed

Sacrament. In my free time, I would go there to pray, and often my eyes would be drawn toward a beautiful image of Our Lord's foster father, an image greatly venerated in that church, where I once conducted a retreat for attorneys. I have always liked to think of Saint Joseph in the setting of the Holy Family: Jesus, Mary, and Joseph. I used to pray to all three of them for help with various problems. I can well understand the unity and love that characterized the Holy Family: three hearts, one love. I entrusted the Family Apostolate to Saint Joseph's particular care.

In Kraków, at Podgórze, there is another church dedicated to Saint Joseph. I often went there during pastoral visitations. The shrine of Saint Joseph in Kalisz is of exceptional importance. Priests who are former prisoners of Dachau make pilgrimages of gratitude there. A group of them, while prisoners in this Nazi concentration camp, entrusted themselves to the care of Saint Joseph and they were saved. On their return to Poland, they began making an annual pilgrimage of thanksgiving to the shrine at Kalisz, and they always invited me to join them. This group included Archbishop Kazimierz Majdański, Bishop Ignacy Jeż, and Cardinal Adam Kozłowiecki, a missionary in Africa.

Divine providence prepared Saint Joseph to be the foster father of Jesus Christ. In the Apostolic Exhortation dedicated to him, *Redemptoris Custos*, I wrote: "As can be deduced from the gospel texts, Joseph's marriage to Mary is the juridical basis of his fatherhood. It was to assure fatherly protection for Jesus that God chose Joseph to be Mary's spouse. It follows that Joseph's fatherhood—a relationship that places him as close as possible to Christ, to whom every election and predestination is ordered (*cf. Rom. 8:28–29*)—comes to pass through marriage to Mary" (n. 7). Joseph was called to be Mary's most chaste spouse precisely in order to be a father to Jesus. The fatherhood of Saint Joseph, like the motherhood of the Blessed Virgin Mary, has a fundamentally Christological character. All Mary's privileges flow from the fact that she is Christ's mother. In like manner, all Saint Joseph's privileges flow from the fact that he was chosen to act as father to Christ.

We know that Jesus addressed God with the word *"Abba"*—a loving, familiar word that would have been used by children in first-century Palestine when speaking to their fathers. Most probably Jesus, like other children, used this same word when speaking to Saint Joseph. Can any more be said about the mystery of human fatherhood? Jesus Himself, as a man, experienced the fatherhood of God through that father–son relationship with Saint Joseph. This filial encounter with Joseph then fed into Our Lord's revelation of the paternal name of God. What a profound mystery!

Christ in His divinity had His own experience of divine fatherhood and sonship within the Most Holy Trinity. In His humanity, He experienced sonship thanks to Saint Joseph. For his part, Saint Joseph offered the child growing up beside him the support of a healthy masculinity, a clear understanding of human problems, and courage. He fulfilled this role aided by the qualities of the best of fathers, drawing strength from that supreme source from which *"every family in heaven and on earth is named" (Eph. 3:15)*. Humanly speaking, he taught the Son of God many things, and provided Him with an earthly home.

For Saint Joseph, life with Jesus was a continuous discovery of his own vocation as a father. He became a father in an extraordinary way, without begetting his son in the flesh. Isn't this, perhaps, an example of the type of fatherhood that is proposed to us, priests and bishops, as a model? Everything I did in the course of my ministry I saw as an expression of this kind of fatherhood—baptizing, hearing confessions, celebrating the Eucharist, preaching, admonishing, encouraging. For me these things were always a way of living out that fatherhood.

We should think particularly of the home Saint Joseph built for the Son of God when we touch upon the subject of priestly and episcopal celibacy. Celibacy, in fact, provides the fullest opportunity to live out this type of fatherhood: chaste and totally dedicated to Christ and His Virgin Mother. Unconstrained by any personal solicitude for a family, a priest can dedicate himself *with his whole heart* to his pastoral responsibilities. One can therefore understand the tenacity with which the Latin Church has defended the tradition of celibacy for its priests, resisting the pressures that have arisen from time to time throughout history. This tradition is clearly demanding, but it has yielded particularly rich spiritual fruit. At the same time, it is a source of joy to recognize the fine examples of pastoral zeal offered by the married priesthood of the Eastern Catholic Churches. In the struggle against communism, in particular, married Eastern-rite priests have proved just as heroic as their celibate counterparts. As Cardinal Josyf Slipyj once observed, both celibate and married clergy showed great courage when faced with the communists.

It is important to point out that there are profound theological reasons supporting the discipline of celibacy. The encyclical *Sacerdotalis Caelibatus*, published in 1967 by my venerable predecessor Pope Paul VI, synthesizes them as follows (cf. nn. 19–34).

• First and foremost there is a *Christological motivation*: as Mediator between the Father and the human race, Christ remained celibate so as to dedicate Himself totally to the service of God and men. Those whose fortune it is to share in the dignity and mission of Christ are called to share also in this total gift of self.
• Then there is an *ecclesiological motivation*: Christ loved the Church, offering Himself entirely for her

sake, in order to make her a glorious, holy, and immaculate Spouse. By choosing celibacy, the sacred ministers themselves manifest the virginal love of Christ for the Church, drawing forth the supernatural vigor of spiritual fruitfulness.

• Finally there is an *eschatological* motivation: at the resurrection of the dead, Jesus said, *"they neither marry nor are given in marriage, but are like angels in heaven" (Matt. 22:30)*. Priestly celibacy proclaims the arrival of a new dawn of salvation, and in a way it anticipates the fulfillment of the kingdom as it sets forth its supreme values that will one day shine forth in all the children of God.

Some, seeking to argue against the discipline of celibacy, draw attention to the loneliness of a priest or a bishop. On the basis of my own experience, I firmly reject this argument. Personally, I have never felt lonely. Aside from constant awareness that the Lord is close at hand, I have always been surrounded by people, and I have maintained cordial relations with priests—deans, pastors, assistant pastors—and with all kinds of lay people.

Being with One's People

We should also think of the home Saint Joseph built for the Son of God when we speak of the bishop's paternal duty to be with the people entrusted to his care. The bishop's home is, in fact, his diocese. This is true not only because he lives and works there but also in a much deeper sense: The bishop's home is the diocese because it is the place where he must daily manifest his fidelity to the Church—his Bride. When the Council of Trent, addressing long-standing abuses in this area, defined and underlined the bishop's obligation to be resident in his diocese, it was also expressing a profound insight: the bishop must be with his Church at all important moments. He should never leave it for longer than a month, unless he has a serious reason.

Like a good "paterfamilias," he is constantly with his family, and if ever he has to be away from them, he misses them and wants to return to them as soon as possible.

In this connection, I would like to recall the faithful bishop of Tarnów, Bishop Jerzy Ablewicz. The priests of his diocese knew that he did not receive visitors on Fridays. On that day he would make the pilgrimage on foot to the Marian shrine at Tuchów. Along the way he would prayerfully prepare his Sunday homily. It was well known that he was loath to leave his diocese. He was always with his people, firstly in prayer and then in action. But prayer always came first. The mystery of our fatherhood begins with prayer and grows from prayer. As men of faith, we present ourselves in prayer before Mary and Joseph to ask for their assistance; in this way, together with them and with all those whom God entrusts to us, we can build a home for the Son of God—His Holy Church.

The Chapel at 3 Franciszkańska Street

The chapel in the episcopal residence in Kraków has a very particular significance for me: it is the place where I was ordained a priest by Cardinal Sapieha on November 1, 1946, even though ordinations usually took place in the cathedral. The place and the date of my priestly ordination were influenced by my Ordinary's decision to send me to Rome to study.

Toward the end of his life, Saint Paul, by now an experienced Apostle, wrote to Timothy: *"Train yourself in devotion, for, while physical training is of limited value, devotion is valuable in every respect, since it holds a promise of life both for the present and for the future"* (1 Tim. 4: 7–8). Every bishop enjoys the privilege of maintaining a chapel in his own home, so close that he can reach out and touch it, but this privilege also brings with it great responsibility. The reason for having a chapel so close is so that everything in the bishop's life—his teaching, his decisions, his pastoral care—might begin from the feet of Christ, concealed in the Blessed Sacrament. I witnessed firsthand the habitual practice of Cardinal Adam Sapieha in this regard. In his homily at Cardinal Sapieha's funeral, Cardinal Wyszyński said: "One aspect of this man's life, one among many others, has caused me to reflect. At the end of a long and exhausting working day during the meetings of the Episcopal Conference, the rest of us were all tired and would hurry back home. He, however, seemingly indefatigable, would go to his cold chapel and stay there in the presence of God until late at night. For how long? I don't know. I never heard the footsteps of the Cardinal coming back from the chapel, while I was working late nights at the archbishop's residence. One thing I do know: at his advanced age he was entitled to some rest. I think the Cardinal needed to conclude his daily labors with the golden lock of sleep and instead he closed them with the diamond of prayer. This was truly a man of prayer!"[21]

I tried to imitate his unparalleled example by not only praying in the house chapel but also sitting, writing my books there. That's where I wrote *Person and Action,* among others. I have always been convinced that the chapel is a place of special inspiration. What a great privilege to be able to live and work in the shadow of His Presence, such a powerfully magnetic Presence! My dear deceased friend, André Frossard, captured something of the power and the beauty of this Presence in his book *God Exists: I've Met Him*. It is not always necessary to enter physically into the chapel in order to enter spiritually into the presence of the Blessed Sacrament. I have always sensed that Christ was the real owner of my episcopal residence, and that we bishops are just short-term tenants. That's how it was in Franciszkańska Street for almost twenty years, and that's how it is here in the Vatican.

EPISCOPAL COLLEGIALITY

"He appointed twelve, to be with him and to be sent out to preach" (Mark 3:14)

The Bishop in His Diocese

The Second Vatican Council provided me with a strong impulse to intensify pastoral activity. This, of course, is where everything should begin. On June 3, 1963, Pope John XXIII died. It was he who had summoned the Council, which opened on October 11, 1962. I was privileged to have taken part in it from the very beginning. The first session opened during October and ended on December eighth. I was present at the sessions with the council fathers as vicar capitular of the archdiocese of Kraków.

After the death of John XXIII, the Conclave elected as Pope the archbishop of Milan, Cardinal Giovanni Battista Montini, on June 21, 1963. He took the name of Paul VI. In the fall of that same year, the Council entered its second session, during which I was again present in the same capacity. On January 13, 1964, I was named metropolitan archbishop of Kraków. The nomination was published shortly thereafter, and on March eighth, Laetare Sunday, I solemnly took possession of the see in Wawel Cathedral.

On the threshold I was welcomed by Professor Franciszek Bielak and Monsignor Bohdan Niemczewski, the mitred provost of the chapter. Then I entered the cathedral, where I was to occupy the episcopal throne left vacant after the deaths of Cardinal Sapieha and Archbishop Baziak. I do not remember the details of the address I delivered on that occasion, but I do remember that my thoughts were filled with the emotion I felt for Wawel Cathedral and its cultural heritage, to which I have forever felt bound, as I have stressed earlier.

The Pallium

I also remember the profound and touching sign of the pallium, which I received in that same year, 1964. Throughout the world, metropolitans, as a symbol of their union with Christ the Good Shepherd and with His vicar the Successor of Peter, wear around their necks this sign made from the wool of sheep blessed on the feast of Saint Agnes. On so many occasions during my pontificate, on the feast of the Holy Apostles Peter and Paul, I have been able to confer it upon new metropolitans. What wonderful symbolism! We can recognize in this simple sign the image of a sheep that the Good Shepherd places on his shoulders and carries with him, to save it and to feed it. It is a symbol that makes visible something that unites all bishops: our solicitude and responsibility for the flock entrusted to us. It is precisely because of this solicitude and responsibility that we are given the task of cultivating and safeguarding unity.

After March 8, 1964, the day of my installation, I took part in the Council as a metropolitan archbishop until its conclusion on December 8, 1965. The experience of the Council, those faith-filled encounters with the bishops of the universal Church and, at the same time, the new responsibility entrusted to me in relation to the archdiocese of Kraków, all helped me to understand more profoundly the place of a bishop within the Church.

The Bishop in His Local Church

What is the place that God in His goodness assigns to a bishop within the Church? From the outset, as one belonging to the apostolic succession, he sees before him the universal Church. He is sent out *into the whole world* and, precisely for this reason, he becomes a sign of the catholicity of the Church. I have been aware of this universal dimension of the Church since my earliest childhood, ever since I first learned to recite the words of the creed: "I believe in one holy catholic and apostolic Church." It is this universal community that embraces the witness of so many times, places, and people, all those chosen by God and gathered together into one, "from the time of Adam, from Abel the just one, to the last of the elect" (*Lumen Gentium, 2*). This great witness and these bonds of fellowship are eloquently expressed in the liturgy of episcopal ordination, so as to call to mind the entire history of salvation with its proper end, which is the unity of all people in God.

Every bishop, while he bears within himself a responsibility for the universal Church, finds himself placed at the center of a particular Church, namely the community that Christ has entrusted specifically to him, so that through his episcopal ministry the mystery of the Church of Christ, the sign of salvation for all people, may be realized ever more perfectly. In the Dogmatic Constitution *Lumen Gentium*, we read: "This Church of Christ is really present in all legitimately organized local groups of the faithful, which, insofar as they are united to their pastors, are also quite appropriately called Churches in the New Testament. . . . In each community gathered around the altar, under the sacred ministry of the bishop, a manifest symbol is to be seen of that charity and 'unity of the mystical body, without which there can be no salvation.' In these communities, though they may often be small and poor, or existing in the diaspora, Christ is present through whose power and influence the One, Holy, Catholic and Apostolic Church is constituted" (n. 26).

The mystery of the bishop's vocation in the Church consists precisely in the fact that he is situated both in this particular visible community, for which he was made a bishop, and at the same time in the universal

Church. It is important to understand clearly the singular connection between these two aspects. It would undoubtedly be an oversimplification and a serious misunderstanding of the mystery to think that the bishop *represents* the universal Church in his own diocesan community—in my case, Kraków—and, at the same time, *represents* this to the universal Church, in the way in that, for example, ambassadors represent their respective states or international organizations.

The bishop is the sign of Christ's presence in the world, going out to meet men and women where they are: calling them by name, helping them to rise, consoling them with the Good News and gathering them into one around the Lord's Table. For this reason, the bishop, while belonging to the whole world and to the universal Church, lives out his vocation physically removed from the other members of the Episcopal College, so as to be close to the people whom, in Christ's name, he calls together in his particular Church. At the same time, he becomes for these very people a sign that their isolation is ended, because he brings them into fellowship with Christ and, in Him, with all those whom God chose beforehand since the world began, with those whom He calls together today throughout the world, and with those whom He will call into His Church in the future, until the very last of the elect. All are present in the local Church through the ministry and the sign of the bishop.

The bishop exercises his ministry in a truly responsible way when he is able to call forth in his people a lively sense of communion with himself and, through his person, with all believers throughout the world. In Kraków, I had personal experience of this living sense of unity in the hearts of priests, religious orders, and the laity. May God reward them! Saint Augustine, seeking help and understanding, was accustomed to say to the faithful: "There are many people who reach God as Christians without being in charge of anything, and no doubt have all the easier a journey for traveling light, and carrying less of a burden. But we bishops, apart from being Christians, as which we shall render God an account of our manner of life, are also in charge of you, and as such will render God an account of our stewardship."[22]

This is the mystery of the mystical encounter with men *"from every nation, race, people and language" (Rev. 7:9)*, with Christ present in the diocesan bishop, around whom the local Church is gathered at a specific moment in history. What a strong union this is! With what magnificent bonds they are united and held together! I experienced this during the Council. In a particular way, I experienced collegiality: the entire episcopate with Peter! I relived this experience afresh in 1976, when I preached the retreat to the Roman Curia, assembled around Pope Paul VI. But I shall return to this later.

Collegiality

Let us cast our minds back to the beginnings of the Church when, by the will of our Lord and Master, the apostolic office was instituted. The community of *"those whom he wanted" (cf. Mark 3:13)* grew around Him. Within that group, different personalities were formed and deepened, beginning with Simon Peter. It is into this college of disciples and friends of Christ that every new bishop is introduced, through the call and the consecration that he receives. The college! Our participation in this community of faith, of witness, of love, and of responsibility is the gift that we receive together with our call and our consecration. What a wonderful gift it is!

We bishops all find that the presence of our brothers provides us with support expressed through the bonds of prayer and ministry, through our witnesss, and through sharing the fruits of our pastoral labors. A particular comfort for me today, from this point of view, are the meetings and exchanges that I have with bishops during their visits *ad limina Apostolorum*. My great desire is that the workings of God's grace in their hearts, minds, and actions should be recognized and cherished by all. Today's rapid communications make it possible to meet more often and more fruitfully. This enables each of us, bishops in the Catholic Church, to look for ways to reinforce our episcopal collegiality, including active collaboration within Episcopal Conferences and joint discussion of our experiences within the great family of the Church throughout the world. If bishops meet together and confide in one another their joys and their concerns, this will surely help them to maintain that "spirituality of communion" of which I wrote in the Apostolic Letter *Novo millennio ineunte* (cf. nn. 43–45).

Even before my election to the See of Peter, I met numerous bishops from every country, although, naturally enough, I saw more of the bishops from neighboring European countries. These meetings were a source of mutual comfort. At times, especially when the bishops were from countries under a communist dictatorship, they could be quite dramatic. I am thinking, for example, of the funeral of Cardinal Stefan Trochta in the then Czechoslovakia, when contact with the local Church was either impeded or made outright impossible by the communist authorities.

Before the cardinals decided that I should be the one to occupy the See of Peter, my last pastoral encounter with bishops from a neighboring country was in Germany, where I went together with Primate Wyszyński in September 1978. This was an important sign of reconciliation between the two nations. All these meetings have been continued in an extraordinarily intense way in the daily meetings with bishops from various parts of the world that I have been privileged to experience since my election to the Chair of Saint Peter.

The visits *ad limina Apostolorum* are a particular expression of collegiality. On principle, every five years (sometimes there can be delays), bishops from more than two thousand dioceses all over the world take it in turns to come to the Vatican. Now it is my turn to receive them, just as I was received at the time of Paul VI. I greatly appreciated my meetings with Paul VI, from whom I learned a great deal about how to structure these visits and how to conduct them. Now I have devised a pattern of my own: Firstly I receive each bishop personally, then I invite the group to lunch, and finally we celebrate morning Mass together and have our formal group meeting.

I draw great profit from meeting bishops: I could say in all simplicity that from them I learn about the Church. I need to do this constantly, because I am always learning new things. From my conversations with them I come to know about the situation of the Church in different parts of the world: in Europe, in Asia, in America, in Africa, and in Oceania.

The Lord has given me the strength to be able to visit most of these countries. This is very important, because to spend time personally in a country, even if only briefly, allows one to see all sorts of things. Besides, these meetings allow me to establish direct contact with the people, and this has great value both at the interpersonal and at the ecclesial level. It was the same for Saint Paul, who was constantly traveling. Precisely for this reason, as one reads his letters to different Christian communities, one senses that he lived among them, that he knew the people of each locality and their problems. The same is true at every stage in history, including our own.

I have always enjoyed traveling, and I am convinced that this task has in a sense been given to the Pope by Christ Himself. Even while I was a diocesan bishop I enjoyed pastoral visitations and I considered it very important to be aware of what was happening in the parishes, to know the people and to meet them directly. While it is true that pastoral visitations are a canonical requirement, experience of life would be enough to recommend them. Saint Paul is the model here. Peter too, but Paul first and foremost.

The Council Fathers

During the first session of the Council, when I was still an auxiliary bishop in the archdiocese of Kraków, I had occasion to thank Cardinal Giovanni Battista Montini for the generous and valuable gift that the archdiocese of Milan had made to the collegiate church of Saint Florian in Kraków: three new bells (a symbolic and most eloquent gift, not least because of the names given to the bells: Virgin Mary, Ambrose-Charles Borromeo, and Florian). Father Tadeusz Kurowski, provost of the collegiate church of Saint Florian, had requested them, and Archbishop Montini, always very generous toward the Polish people, took the project to his heart and showed great understanding toward me, a very young bishop at the time.

My Italian colleagues, who took charge, so to speak, of the council proceedings and the work of the Vatican in general, always astounded me by their courtesy and their sense of the universal Church. During the first session, the universality of the Church was brought home to me in an extraordinary way by my contact with a number of bishops from Africa. They were distributed throughout Saint Peter's Basilica, where, as everyone knows, the work of the Council unfolded, and among them were some eminent theologians and zealous pastors. They had plenty to say. More than anyone else, Archbishop Raymond-Marie Tchidimbo of Conakry left an impression on me; he suffered greatly at the hands of the communist president of his country and was eventually forced into exile. I had cordial and frequent contact with Cardinal Hyacinthe Thiandoum, an exceptional personality. Another eminent figure was Cardinal Paul Zoungrana. Both men were formed in French culture, and spoke that language as if it were their mother tongue. I established a close friendship with these two prelates when I lived in the Polish College.

I also felt very close to the French cardinal, Gabriel-Marie Garrone, twenty years my senior. He was extremely courteous toward me, I might even say affectionate. We were made cardinals together, and after the Council he became prefect of the Congregation for Catholic Education. I seem to remember that he also took part in the conclave. Another Frenchman with whom I established a close friendship was the theologian Henri de Lubac, S.J., whom I myself, years later, made a cardinal.

The Council was a privileged period for becoming acquainted with bishops and theologians, above all in the individual commissions. When Schema 13 was being studied (later to become the Pastoral Constitution on the Church in the modern world, *Gaudium et spes*), and I spoke on personalism, Father de Lubac came to me and said, encouragingly: "Yes, yes, yes, that's the way forward," and this meant a great deal to me, as I was still relatively young.

I also established friendships with Germans: Cardinal Alfred Bengsch, a year my junior, Joseph Höffner of Cologne, and Joseph Ratzinger, churchmen of exceptional theological competence. I particularly remember the then very young Professor Ratzinger. At the Council he was accompanying Cardinal Joseph Frings, archbishop of Cologne, as a theological expert. He was later named archbishop of Munich by Pope Paul VI, who also made him a cardinal, and he took part in the conclave that elected me to the Petrine ministry. When Cardinal Franjo Šeper died, I asked Cardinal Ratzinger to take his place as prefect of the Congregation for the Doctrine of the Faith. I thank God for the presence and the assistance of this great man, who is a trusted friend.

Unfortunately very few of the bishops and cardinals who took part in the Second Vatican Council (October 11, 1962–December 8, 1965) are still alive. It was a most wonderful ecclesial event, and I thank God that I was able to participate in it from the first day to the last.

The College of Cardinals

In a certain sense, the heart of the Episcopal College is the College of Cardinals, who surround the successor of Peter and sustain him in his witness of faith before the whole Church. I became a member of this College in June 1967.

The gathering of cardinals is a particularly visible expression of the principle of collaboration and mutual support in faith on which the Church's whole missionary endeavor is built. Peter's task is the one assigned to him by Jesus: *"And you, when you have turned again, strengthen your brethren" (Luke 22:32)*. From the earliest centuries, the successors of Peter have availed themselves of the collaboration of the College of bishops, priests, and deacons, who shared in their responsibility for the city of Rome and for the neighboring dioceses (the so-called suburbicarian sees). They began to be designated as *viri cardinales*. Obviously, as the centuries have gone by, the forms of this cooperation have changed, but their essential significance remains unchanged, as a sign for the Church and for the world.

Since the pastoral responsibility of the successor of Peter extends to the whole world, it has become increasingly opportune that all over the Christian world, *viri cardinales* should be present, particularly close to Peter both in sharing his responsibility and in their total readiness to witness to the faith, even to the shedding of their blood (hence they wear scarlet, like the blood of the martyrs). I give thanks to God for the support and the sharing in responsibility for Church government that the cardinals of the Roman Curia and throughout the world so generously offer me. The readier they are to support others, the more they confirm them in their faith and, in consequence, the more able they are to fulfill the enormous responsibility of electing, under the guidance of the Holy Spirit, the one who is to assume the Office of Peter.

Synods

My life as a bishop began at almost the same time as the announcement of the forthcoming Council. As is well known, one of the fruits of the Council was the institution of the Synod of Bishops, created by Pope Paul VI on September 15, 1965. Since then, several Synods have taken place. An important role in their planning and execution falls to the general secretary. The first to hold this office was Cardinal Władysław Rubin, whose wartime adventures brought him via Lebanon to Rome. Paul VI entrusted him with the creation of the Synod secretariat, no easy task. I did what I could to support him, principally by offering advice. Later he was succeeded by Cardinal Jozef Tomko, who in turn was followed by Cardinal Jan Pieter Schotte.

As I mentioned, there have been several Synods. Besides those celebrated under Paul VI, there have been Synods on the family, on the sacrament of reconciliation and penance, on the role of the laity in the life of the Church, on priestly formation, on consecrated life, on the episcopate. There have also been some with more specific themes: one for the Netherlands, one for the twentieth anniversary of the conclusion of the Second Vatican Council, and one for the Special Assembly for Lebanon. Then there have been the Synods on the various continents: Africa, Americas, Asia, Oceania, and two Synods for Europe. The idea was to cover all the continents before the new millennium, to come to know them and to note their problems, in preparation for the Great Jubilee. This program was carried out. Now our thoughts must turn to the next Synod, on the sacrament of the Eucharist.

As a bishop, I had already had experience of a Synod—a most important one had taken place in the archdiocese of Kraków, to mark the nine-hundredth anniversary of Saint Stanislaus. Obviously this was just a diocesan Synod, concerned not with the affairs of the universal Church, but with the far more modest situation of the local Church. Nevertheless, diocesan Synods are also significant for a community of the faithful who live day by day the same problems associated with the practice of the faith in specific social and political circumstances. The task of the Synod of Kraków was to introduce the decisions of the Council into the life of the local community. I planned this Synod for the period 1972 to 1979 because, as I mentioned earlier, Saint Stanislaus was bishop from precisely 1072 to 1079. I wanted those dates to be relived nine hundred years later. The most important experience was the work of the numerous synodal groups, all deeply committed. It was a truly pastoral Synod: bishops, priests, and laity all working together. I concluded this Synod when I was already Pope, during my first journey to Poland.

The Retreat for the Curia During the Pontificate of Paul VI

I shall never forget that truly unique retreat. Making a retreat is a great gift from God. It is the one time when everything else can be put aside so as to encounter God and listen to Him alone. This is without a doubt a most valuable exercise for the retreatant. For that reason, no one should ever be put under pressure to make a retreat, but, if anything, the interior need for it should be awakened. Yes, there are times when one might say to someone: "Go and stay with the Camaldolese or at Tyniec for a break," but in principle, it should really come from an interior need. The Church, as an institution, recommends priests in particular to make retreats, but the canonical norm is just another element along-side the desire arising from the heart.[23]

I have already mentioned that I usually made my retreats at the Benedictine Abbey of Tyniec, but I also often went to the Camaldolese at Bielany, to the Seminary in Kraków, and to the Gray Ursulines at Jaszczurówka (Zakopane). Since I came to Rome, I have made my retreat together with the Curia during the first week of Lent. Over the years, these retreats have always been led by different preachers, some of them magnificent from the point of view of quality of oratory and content, some even for their humor. This was particularly so, for example, in the case of the Jesuit Father Tomáš Špidlik, of Czech origin. We laughed a great deal during his conferences, and this too was beneficial. He knew how to present profound truths in an amusing way, and in this he showed great talent. That retreat came back to my mind when I conferred the Cardinal's hat upon Father Špidlik during the last Consistory. As I said, the preachers have been varied and, in general, excellent. I personally invited Bishop Jerzy Ablewicz, who was the only Pole, apart from myself, to lead the retreat in the Vatican.

When I preached the retreat in the Vatican, it was to Paul VI and his collaborators. During the preparatory phase, there had been a problem. At the beginning of February 1976, I was telephoned by Monsignor Władysław Rubin, who told me that the Pontiff would like me to preach the retreat in March. I had barely three weeks in which to prepare my texts and translate them. The title that I later gave to those meditations was: "Sign of Contradiction." This had not been proposed to me, but it emerged at the end as a kind of synthesis of what I had wanted to say. In reality, it was not a theme, but rather a kind of key concept that tied together everything I had said in the various conferences. I remember the days dedicated to preparing the talks, twenty of them, which I had to choose and put together all by myself. In order to find the necessary peace and quiet, I went to stay with the Gray Ursulines at Jaszczurówka. Until noon I wrote the meditations, then in the afternoon I went skiing, and in the evening I continued writing.

That meeting with Paul VI, in the context of the retreat, was particularly important for me, because it made me realize just how necessary it is for a bishop to be ready to speak of his faith, wherever the Lord asks this of him. Every bishop needs to be prepared for this, including the successor of Peter himself, just as Paul VI needed me to be ready and willing for the task.

The Implementation of the Council

The Council was a wonderful event, and for me it was an unforgettable experience. I returned greatly enriched. When I got back to Poland, I wrote a book in which I presented the insights that had emerged in the course of the conciliar sessions. I tried to capture, so to speak, the juice of the Council's teaching. This volume, entitled *Sources of Renewal: The Implementation of Vatican II*, was originally published in Kraków in 1972 by the Polish Theological Association (PTT). The book was intended as a kind of ex-voto of thanksgiving for what God's grace had given to me personally, as a bishop, through the conciliar experience. The Second Vatican Council, in fact, looks specifically at the responsibilities of the bishop. The First Vatican Council had addressed Papal primacy, but the Second gave particular attention to bishops. To realize this, it is enough to take a look at the documents, above all the Dogmatic Constitution *Lumen Gentium*.

The Council's profound teaching on the episcopate bases itself on Christ's triple function (*munus*) as prophet, priest, and king. The Dogmatic Constitution *Lumen Gentium* examines this in paragraphs 24–27, but other conciliar texts also make reference to these three functions (*tria munera*). Among them, particular attention should be given to the decree *Christus Dominus*, which is concerned specifically with the pastoral office of bishops.

On my return from Rome to Poland, the well-known issue of the Polish bishops' message to the German bishops hit the headlines. In their letter, the Polish bishops, speaking on behalf of the nation, forgave the wrongs they had suffered from the Germans during the Second World War. At the same time, they asked pardon for any wrongs that the Poles might have committed against the Germans. Unfortunately, the message provoked great polemics, accusations, and calumny. This act of reconciliation—which in fact turned out to be decisive for normalizing Polish–German relations—did not go down well with the communist authorities. As a result they became more hostile toward the Church. Obviously this did not make for an ideal situation in which to launch the celebrations of the Millennium of the Baptism of Poland, due to begin at Gniezno in April 1966. In Kraków, the celebrations took place on the feast of Saint Stanislaus, on May eighth. Still today I can vividly recall the spectacle of that multitude of people walking in procession from Wawel to Skałka. The authorities did not feel up to challenging that massive and orderly gathering. During the Millennium celebrations, the tensions created by the bishops' message were dissipated and almost disappeared, and it became possible to proceed with an appropriate catechesis on the significance of the Millennium for the life of the nation.

Another good opportunity for preaching was the annual Corpus Christi procession. Before the war, the great procession in honor of the Body and Blood of Christ made its way from Wawel Cathedral as far as Rynek Główny, across the streets and squares of the city. During the German occupation, the governor Hans Frank prohibited it. Later, during the communist period, the authorities allowed it once again, but with a shorter route: from Wawel Cathedral around the courtyard of the royal castle. Only in 1971 was the procession once again allowed to go outside Wawel itself. At that time I tried to base the themes of the addresses I would give at each of the various altars not only on Eucharistic catechesis, but also on different aspects of the great question of *religious liberty*, so very topical at that moment.

I believe that in these multiple forms of popular piety lies hidden the answer to a question that is sometimes raised concerning the significance of such manifestations of local tradition. The answer is simple: when hearts are united, the result is a great force for good. To be rooted in what is ancient, strong, profound, and, at the same time, dear to the heart, gives an extraordinary interior energy. If this rootedness is then joined by a bold and strong intellectual dimension, there is no need to fear for the future of the faith or the prospect for human relationships within the nation. Amid the rich *humus* of tradition, in fact, culture is nourished and this unites the citizens, enabling them to live together as a great family, sustaining and strengthening their convictions. Our great task, especially today, in the age of so-called globalization, is to cultivate sound traditions so as to promote a bold consensus in thought and imagination, an openness toward the future and at the same time an affectionate respect for the past. It is a past that endures in human hearts in the form of ancient words, ancient signs, memories, and customs inherited from previous generations.

The Polish Bishops

During my ministry in Kraków, I had particularly friendly relationships with three bishops of Gorzów: Wilhelm Pluta, now a Servant of God, Jerzy Stroba, and Ignacy Jeż. I regarded them as real friends and so I would seek them out, even aside from official business. Stroba and I had known one another in Kraków, where he had been rector of the Silesian Seminary. I had been a professor in that seminary myself, teaching ethics, fundamental moral theology, and social ethics. Of the three, only Bishop Ignacy Jeż is still alive. He is gifted with a lively sense of humor, which he demonstrates, for example, by making jokes about his own surname ("Jeż" in Polish means "hedgehog").

As a residential bishop, I had some auxiliary bishops

in my archdiocese: Julian Groblicki, Jan Pietraszko, Stanisław Smoleński, and Albin Małysiak (the last two, as I have mentioned, I ordained personally). I appreciated Bishop Małysiak's energy. I remember him when he was still a pastor in Nowa Wieś, a district of Kraków. Sometimes I liked to call him Albin the Zealot. Bishop Jan Pietraszko was a magnificent preacher, a man who could generate real enthusiasm in his listeners. In 1994, Cardinal Franciszek Macharski, my successor as archbishop, was able to begin the process of his beatification. Now the process has arrived in Rome. I have happy memories also of the other two auxiliaries: for years we worked together in order to serve our beloved Church of Kraków, in a spirit of fraternal communion.

In nearby Tarnów, there was Bishop Jerzy Ablewicz, whom I have already mentioned. I often went to see him. We were close in age; he was just one year older.

The bishop of Częstochowa, Stefan Bareła, treated me with great kindness. On the twenty-fifth anniversary of his priestly ordination, I said the following during the homily: "The episcopate is like a further and, in some sense, a new discovery of priesthood. Both must be lived according to the same criterion: always focusing on Christ, the one Shepherd and pastor of our souls. A bishop must focus on Christ even more profoundly, more ardently, more resolutely. He carries out his mission by focusing also on souls, immortal souls, redeemed by the Blood of Christ. This focus on souls is perhaps not as immediate as it would be in the daily ministry of a priest in a parish, as pastor or assistant pastor. On the other hand, it is with a broader perspective, since it is the entire community of the Church that a bishop sees before him. We bishops of the Second Vatican Council recognize that the Church is the locus which gathers together the entire human family, it is the place of reconciliation, bringing people together no matter what, it is the place of convergence through dialogue, of convergence even at the cost of personal suffering. It may be that for us, Polish bishops at the time of the Second Vatican Council, it is more about suffering than about dialogue."[24]

In Silesia, there was Bishop Herbert Bednorz, and before him, Bishop Stanisław Adamski. Bishop Bednorz became his coadjutor. When I was made metropolitan, I went to see all the bishops of the province, and this included a trip to Katowice to see Bishop Adamski. He had with him Bishops Julian Bieniek and Józef Kurpas. I got on well with the bishops of Silesia. I used to meet them regularly on the last Sunday in May at the Shrine of Our Lady of Piekary, the day when the great pilgrimage of miners would arrive there. Bishop Bednorz would constantly invite me to preach. The last Sunday in May, in fact, was quite an occasion: this pilgrimage took on a particular character in the context of the People's Republic of Poland. All those present would listen out for the homily and would strongly applaud every sentence that contained a challenge to any controversial aspect of government policy regarding religion or morals, for example the matter of Sunday observance. In this connection, a saying of Bishop Bednorz became popular in Silesia: "Sunday belongs to God and to us." At the end of the celebrations, Bishop Bednorz used to turn to me with these words: "So we look forward to next year for another homily like that one." The miners of Piekary, with their magnificent pilgrimage, remain for me a remarkable witness, something altogether extraordinary.

A particular place in my heart belongs to Andrzej Maria Deskur, now President Emeritus of the Pontifical Council for Social Communications, whom I made a cardinal on May 25, 1985. He has often assisted me since the very beginning of my pontificate, especially through his suffering, but also with his wise counsel.

As I recall these bishops, I cannot omit to mention my great patron, Saint Charles Borromeo. Whenever I think of him, I am struck by the coincidence of facts and responsibilities. He was a bishop in sixteenth-century Milan, at the time of the Council of Trent. The Lord called me to be a bishop in the twentieth century, at the time of the Second Vatican Council, and we were both entrusted with a similar task relative to those councils—their implementation. I must say that over the years of my pontificate, the implementation of the

Council has constantly remained at the forefront of my thoughts. I have always been impressed by this coincidence, and what particularly fascinates me about that saintly bishop is his enormous pastoral zeal: after the Council, Saint Charles dedicated himself to pastoral visits in the diocese, which at that time included about eight hundred parishes. The archdiocese of Kraków was smaller, yet I did not succeed in completing the round of visits that I began. My present diocese of Rome is also large: it contains 333 parishes. So far I have been to 317: so there are another sixteen left to visit.

GOD AND COURAGE

"Here I am, I come to do your will" (Heb. 10:7)

Courageous in Faith

I remember the words spoken by Cardinal Stefan Wyszyński on May 11, 1946, the day before his episcopal ordination at Jasna Góra: "Being a bishop has something of the Cross about it, which is why the Church places the Cross on the bishop's breast. On the Cross, we have to die to ourselves; without this there cannot be the fullness of the priesthood. To take up one's Cross is not easy, even if it is made of gold and studded with jewels." Ten years later, on March 16, 1956, he said: "The bishop has the duty to serve not only through his words and through the liturgy, but also through offering up his sufferings." Cardinal Wyszyński returned to these thoughts again on another occasion: "Lack of courage in a bishop is the beginning of disaster. Can he still be an apostle? Witnessing to the Truth is essential for an apostle. And this always demands courage."[25]

These words are also his: "The greatest weakness in an apostle is fear. What gives rise to fear is lack of confidence in the power of the Lord; this is what oppresses the heart and tightens the throat. The apostle then ceases to offer witness. Does he remain an apostle? The disciples who abandoned the Master increased the courage of the executioners. Silence in the presence of the enemies of a cause encourages them. Fear in an apostle is the principal ally of the enemies of the cause. 'Use fear to enforce silence' is the first goal in the strategy of the wicked. The terror used in all dictatorships depends on the fearfulness of apostles. Silence possesses apostolic eloquence only when it does not turn its face away from those who strike it. So it was in the case of Christ's silence. But in that sign, he demonstrated his own courage. Christ did not allow himself to be terrorized. Going out to the crowd, he said courageously: 'I am he.'"[26]

Truly, there can be no turning one's back upon the truth, ceasing to proclaim it, hiding it, even if it is a hard truth that can only be revealed at the cost of great suffering. *"You will know the truth, and the truth will set you free" (John 8:32)*: this is our duty and our source of strength! Here there is no room for compromise nor for an opportunistic recourse to human diplomacy. We have to bear witness to the truth, even at the cost of persecutions, even to the shedding of our blood, like Christ Himself and like my saintly predecessor in Kraków, Bishop Stanislaus of Szczepanów.

We will certainly encounter trials. There is nothing extraordinary about this, it is part of the life of faith. At times our trials will be light, at times they will be very difficult, or even dramatic. In our trials we may feel alone, but God's grace, the grace of a victorious faith, will never abandon us. Therefore we can expect to triumph over every trial, even the hardest.

When I spoke about this on June 12, 1987, at Westerplatte in Gdansk to Polish young people, I spoke of that place as an eloquent symbol of fidelity in the face of a dramatic challenge. There it was, in 1939, that a group of young Polish soldiers, fighting against the decidedly superior and better equipped forces of the German invaders, faced grave danger as they bore a victorious witness of courage, perseverance, and fidelity. I referred to that episode, inviting the young people to reflect, above all, on the relation "between *being more* and *having more*," and I warned them: "*Having more* must never be allowed to win. If it did, we would lose the most precious gift of all: our humanity, our conscience, our dignity." In this vein, I encouraged them: "You must make demands on yourselves, even if others do not make demands on you." And I went on to explain: "Each of you, young people, will experience a

'Westerplatte' of your own: responsibilities that you must assume and fulfill, a just cause, for which you must fight, a duty, an obligation, from which there can be no withdrawal, no running away. A system of truths and values that must be 'upheld' and 'defended': a Westerplatte in you and around you. Yes, defend these things for yourselves and for others."

People have always needed models to imitate, and that need is all the greater today, amid such a welter of confusing and conflicting ideas.

The Saints of Kraków

Speaking of models to imitate, we must not overlook the saints. What a great gift it is for a diocese to have its own saints and its own blesseds. What a moving experience for a bishop to be able to present as models for the faithful specific individuals who have distinguished themselves through their exemplary lives of heroic faith and virtue. It is all the more moving when the people concerned lived in recent times. I had the joy of initiating the canonization process for outstanding Christians associated with the Kraków archdiocese. Later, as the bishop of Rome, I was able to confirm their heroic virtues and, once the entire process had been concluded, to raise them to the altars as saints and as blesseds.

During the Second World War, I worked as a laborer in the Solvay factory, near the monastery of Łagiewniki. I often visited the grave of Sister Faustina, who at that time was not yet beatified. Everything about her was extraordinary, impossible to foresee in such a simple girl. How could I have imagined that one day I would beatify her and canonize her? She entered the convent in Warsaw, and was later sent to Vilnius, and finally to Kraków. A few years before the war, she had a great vision of the merciful Jesus, who called her to be the apostle of the devotion to the Divine Mercy, later to spread throughout the Church. Sister Faustina died in 1938. Devotion to the Divine Mercy began in Kraków, and from there took on a worldwide dimension. When I became archbishop of Kraków, I asked Professor Father Ignacy Różycki to examine her writings. At first he didn't want to, but later he agreed, and went on to make a thorough study of the available documents. Finally he said, "She's a wonderful mystic."

Brother Albert—Adam Chmielowski—occupies a special place in my memory, or rather in my heart. He fought in the January Insurrection, during which a missile wounded his leg. It crippled him, and from then on he wore a prosthesis. He was an outstanding figure for me, and I was spiritually very close to him. I wrote a play about him entitled *Our God's Brother*. His personality fascinated me, and he became a model for me: he gave up art in order to become a servant of the poor, of the "gentlemen of the road." His example helped me to abandon the arts and the theater in order to enter the seminary. Every day I recite the Litany of the Polish Nation, which includes Saint Albert.

Among the saints from Kraków I would like to mention Saint Jacek Odrowąż, whose relics are housed in the church of the Dominicans, where I have often visited. Saint Jacek was a great missionary: from Gdańsk he went eastward all the way to Kiev.

The tomb of Blessed Aniela Salawa, which I often used to visit, is in the church of the Franciscans. She was a simple servant girl, whom I beatified on August 13, 1991, in Kraków. She proved that the work of a servant, fulfilled in a spirit of faith and dedication, can lead to sainthood.

I look to these saints of Kraków as my protectors. There are a great many of them, including Saint Stanislaus; Saint Hedwig; Saint John of Kęty; Saint Casimir, son of the king; and many others. I think of them and pray to them for my country.

The Martyrs

Cross of Christ, may you be forever praised, forever blessed; you are the source of strength and courage, our victory lies in you." I never put on my episcopal pectoral Cross carelessly; I always accompany this gesture with a prayer. It has been resting on my chest, beside my heart, for more than forty-five years. To love the Cross is to love sacrifice. The martyrs are a model for this type of love, for example Bishop Michał Kozal. He was ordained a bishop on August 15, 1939, two weeks before the outbreak of war. He never left his flock even though he knew what price he would have to pay. He died in the Dachau concentration camp, where he was a model and an inspiration to the priests among his fellow prisoners.

In 1999, I beatified 108 martyrs, victims of the Nazis, including three bishops: Archbishop Antoni Julian Nowowiejski of Płock, his auxiliary bishop, Leon Wetmański, and Bishop Władysław Goral of Lublin. Many priests, religious, and laity were raised to the altars with them. How eloquent the unity in faith, in love, and in martyrdom between the pastors and their flock gathered around the Cross of Christ.

The Polish Franciscan, Saint Maximilian Kolbe, is a widely known model of a martyr's loving sacrifice. He gave his life in the Auschwitz concentration camp, offering himself in exchange for a fellow prisoner whom he did not even know—a father of a family.

There are other martyrs closer to our own times. It moves me to remember my meetings with Cardinal François-Xavier Nguyên Van Thuân, who preached the Curial retreat at the Vatican in the Year of the Jubilee. On March 18, 2000, as I thanked him for his meditations, I said: "A witness of the cross in the long years of imprisonment in Vietnam, he has frequently recounted the realities and episodes from his sufferings in prison, thus reinforcing us in the consoling certainty that when everything crumbles around us, and perhaps even within us, Christ remains our unfailing support."

There were so many other strong, steadfast bishops who by their example showed the way for others. . . . What is their common secret? I think it was their courage to live their faith. They gave priority to their faith in their whole life and in everything they did; a bold and fearless faith, a faith strengthened by trials, a faith with the courage to follow generously every call from God—*fortes in fide* . . .

Saint Stanislaus

Standing out against the background of so many illustrious Polish saints, I see the towering figure of Saint Stanislaus, bishop and martyr. As I mentioned, I dedicated a poem to him, in which I spoke of his martyrdom, treating it as a mirror of the history of the Church in Poland. Here is a part of it:

1.

I want to describe the Church, my Church,
born with me, not dying with me—
nor do I die with it,
which always grows beyond me—
the Church: the lowest depth of my existence
and its peak,

the Church—the root which I thrust into
the past and the future alike,
the sacrament of my being in God
who is the Father.

I want to describe the Church,
my Church which bound itself to my land
(this was said: "Whatever you bind on earth
will be bound in heaven"),
thus to my land my Church is bound.
The land lies in the Vistula basin, the tributaries swell
    in spring
when the snows thaw in the Carpathians.
The Church bound itself to my land so that all it binds here
should be bound in heaven.

2.

There was a man; through him my land saw
it was bound to heaven.
There was such a man, there were such people, such
    always are—
Through them the earth sees itself in the sacrament
of a new existence. It is a fatherland,
for here the Father's house is begotten and here is born.
I want to describe my Church in the man whose name was
    Stanislaus.
And King Boleslaus wrote this name with his sword
in the ancient chronicles,

wrote this name with his sword on the cathedral's
marble floor
as the streams of blood were flowing
over the marble floor.

3.

I want to describe the Church in the name
which baptized the nation again
with the baptism of blood,
that it might later pass through the baptism of other
    trials,
through the baptism of desires where the hidden is
    revealed—
the breath of the Spirit;
and in the name which was grafted
on the soil of human freedom earlier than the name
Stanislaus.

4.

At that moment, the Body and the Blood being born
on the soil of human freedom were slashed by the king's
    sword
to the marrow of the priest's word,
slashed at the base of the skull, the living trunk slashed.
The Body and the Blood as yet hardly born,
when the sword struck the metal chalice, and the
    wheaten bread.

5.

The King may have thought: the Church shall not yet be
    born from you,
the nation shall not be born of the word that castigates
the body and the blood;
it will be born of the sword, my sword which severs
your words in midflow,
born from the spilled blood—this the King may have
    thought.
The hidden breath of the Spirit will unify all—
the severed words and the sword, the smashed skull
and the hands dripping with blood—and it says:
go into the future together, nothing shall separate you.
I want to describe my Church in which, for centuries,
the word and the blood go side by side,
united by the hidden breath
of the Spirit.

6.

Stanislaus may have thought: my word will hurt you
and convert,
you will come as a penitent to the cathedral gate,
emaciated by fasting, enlightened by a voice within,
to join the Lord's table like a prodigal son.
If the word did not convert you, the blood will.

The bishop had perhaps no time to think:
let this cup pass from me.

7.

A sword falls on the soil of our freedom.
Blood falls on the soil of our freedom,
And which weighs more?

The first age is at a close,
The second begins.
We take in our hands the outline of the inevitable time.[27]

The Holy Land

I have made many pilgrimages all over the world, but the one I have longed to make for many years now is a pilgrimage in the footsteps of Abraham. Paul VI visited those holy places during his first journey.

I wanted to make my pilgrimage during the Jubilee Year. It would have begun in Ur of the Chaldees, in present-day Iraq, from where Abraham, following God's call, set out so many centuries ago (*cf. Gen. 12:1–3*). Then I wanted to continue toward Egypt, in the footsteps of Moses, who led the Israelites out of that country and received the Ten Commandments on Mount Sinai as the foundation of the covenant with God. Then I would have completed my pilgrimage in the Holy Land, beginning with the site of the Annunciation, then to Bethlehem, the city of the birth of Jesus, and to other places connected with His life and mission.

The journey I made was not exactly as I had originally hoped. I could not follow in the footsteps of Abraham because the Iraqi authorities would not allow me. It was the only place where I was not able to go. I went in spirit to Ur of the Chaldees during a special ceremony organized in the Paul VI Audience Hall. I did go to Egypt, to the foot of Mount Sinai, where God revealed His name to Moses. The Orthodox monks who welcomed us were very hospitable.

Then I went to Bethlehem, Nazareth, and Jerusalem. I visited the Garden of Olives, the Upper Room, and, of course, Calvary, Golgotha. This was my second visit to these holy places. The first time I went there was as archbishop of Kraków during the Council. On the last day of my Jubilee pilgrimage to the Holy Land, I concelebrated Mass at the Holy Sepulchre with Cardinal Angelo Sodano, Secretary of State, and other officials of the Curia. What more can be said? This journey was a wonderful, magnificent experience. Without a doubt, the culminating moment of the pilgrimage was the visit to Calvary, the mount of crucifixion, and to the Sepulchre, that same Sepulchre which was also the scene of the resurrection. My thoughts returned to the emotions I had experienced during my first pilgrimage to the Holy Land. I wrote at the time:

Oh, Holy Land, holy place, what depths you fill within me! That is why I cannot walk on you, I must kneel. So I declare today that an encounter has taken place in you. I kneel—and I set my seal upon you. You will remain here with my seal—you will remain, remain—and I will take you with me, I will transform you in myself into a place of new witness. I leave as a witness who will offer testimony down through the centuries.[28]

The place of redemption! It's not enough to say: "I am glad to have been there." There is something more here: the sign of great suffering, the sign of a redeeming death, the sign of resurrection.

Abraham and Christ: "Here I Am; I Come to Do Your Will" (Heb. 10:7)

The primacy of our faith and the courage that it generates once led each of us *"to obey the call of God and to set out, not knowing where we were to go" (cf. Heb. 11:8)*. The author of the Letter to the Hebrews uses these words in relation to the vocation of Abraham, but they apply to every person's vocation, including the one that is fulfilled in episcopal ministry: the call to primacy in faith and in love. We have been chosen and called *to set out*, but it is not for us to determine *the destination* of our journey. He who ordered us to set out will determine that goal: our faithful God, *the God of the Covenant.*

I recently returned to Abraham in a poetic meditation. Here is an extract:

Abraham, the One who entered the history of man
wants, through you, only to unveil this mystery
hidden from the foundation of the world,
a mystery older than the world!

If today we go to these places
whence, long ago, Abraham set out,
where he heard the Voice, where the promise was
*   fulfilled,*
we do so in order to stand at the threshold—
to go back to the beginning of the Covenant.[29]

In the present meditation on the bishop's vocation, I would like to return to Abraham, our *father in faith,* and especially to the mystery of his encounter with Christ the Savior, who, according to the flesh, is the *"son of Abraham" (Matt. 1:1),* while at the same time He exists *"before Abraham because he is eternal" (cf. John 8:58).* This encounter sheds light upon the mystery of our vocation in faith, and above all, upon our responsibility and the courage that we need in order to fulfill it.

We could describe it as a dual mystery. Above all, it is the mystery of what God's love has already accomplished in human history. At the same time, it is the mystery of the future—that is to say, of hope. The mystery of the threshold we are all called to cross, supported by a faith that never draws back, because we know in whom we have believed (*cf. 2 Tim. 1:12*). This mystery embraces all that was *from the beginning,* that was *before the creation of the world,* and that *is yet to be.* In this way, our faith, our responsibility and our courage take their place within the mysterious fulfillment of God's plan. Our faith, our responsibility and our courage are all necessary if Christ's gift is to manifest itself to the world in all its splendor. Not just the kind of faith that safeguards and keeps intact the treasure of God's mysteries, but a faith that has the courage to open and reveal this treasure in constantly new ways to those to whom Christ sends His disciples. And not just the kind of responsibility that limits itself to defending what has been handed down, but the kind that has the courage to use its talents and multiply them (*cf. Matt 25:14–30*).

Beginning with Abraham, the faith of each of his sons represents a constant leaving behind of what is cherished, familiar, and personal, in order to open up to the unknown, trusting in the truth we share and the common future we all have in God. We are all invited to participate in this process of leaving behind the well-known, the familiar. We are all invited to turn toward the God who, in Jesus Christ, opened Himself to us, *"breaking down the dividing wall of enmity" (Eph. 2:14)* in order to draw us to Himself through the Cross.

In Jesus Christ we see: *fidelity* to the Father's call, *an open heart* for everyone He meets, a *constant journeying* that provides *"nowhere to lay his head" (cf. Matt. 8:20),* and finally *the Cross,* through which to attain the victory of the Resurrection. This is Christ—who goes forward boldly, *allowing nothing to stand in his way* until all is accomplished, *"until He ascends to His Father and our Father" (cf. John 20:17),* the One Who is "the same yesterday, today, and for ever" *(cf. Heb. 13:8).*

Faith in Him, then, is a ceaseless opening up to God's ceaseless overtures into our world, it is our movement towards God, Who for His part leads people towards one another. In this way, all that is mine comes to belong to everyone, while what belongs to others becomes mine also. This is essentially what the father says to the elder brother of the prodigal son: *"Everything I have is yours"* (Luke 15:31). It is significant that these words occur also in the priestly prayer of Jesus, as the Son says to the Father: *"All that is mine is yours and all that is yours is mine"* (John 17:10).

As "His hour" is approaching *(cf. John 7:30; 8:20; 13:1),* Christ Himself speaks of Abraham in words that surprise and startle His listeners: "Abraham your father rejoiced to see my day—he saw it and was glad" (John 8:56). What is the source of Abraham's joy? Is it not the prophetic vision of the love and courage with which *his Son* according to the flesh, our Lord and Savior Jesus, would fulfill the will of His Father to the end? *(cf. Heb. 10:7).* It is in the events of the Passion that we find the most powerful reference to the mystery of Abraham, moved by faith to leave his city and his homeland and set off for the unknown—the same Abraham who, in anguish of heart, leads his long-awaited and dearly beloved son to Mount Moriah to offer him in sacrifice.

When *"His hour"* had come, Jesus said to those who were with Him in the Garden of Gethsemane, to Peter, James, and John, His closest disciples: *"Rise, let us be on our way" (cf. Mark 14:42).* Not only He must "be on his way" to fulfill His Father's will: they, too, must go with Him.

That invitation, *"Rise, let us be on our way,"* is addressed particularly to us bishops, His chosen friends. Even if these words indicate a time of trial, great effort, and a painful cross, we must not allow ourselves to give way to fear. They are also words of peace and joy, the fruit of faith. On another occasion, to the same three disciples, Jesus said: "Rise, and do not be afraid!" (*Matt. 17:7*). God's love does not impose burdens upon us that we cannot carry, nor make demands of us that we cannot fulfill. For whatever He asks of us, He provides the help that is needed.

I say this from the place to which the love of Christ Our Savior has led me, asking of me that I should leave my native land so as to bring forth fruit elsewhere through His grace—fruit that will last (*cf. John 15:16*). Echoing the words of our Lord and Master, I too say to each one of you, dear brothers in the episcopate: *"Rise, let us be on our way!"* Let us go forth full of trust in Christ. He will accompany us as we journey toward the goal that He alone knows.

NOTES

1   *Gift and Mystery: On the Fiftieth Anniversary of My Priestly Ordina-tion,* New York, 1996.

2   "L'Osservatore Romano," English edition, October 22, 2003, p. 3.

3   *The Roman Pontifical,* "Ordination of a Bishop," Prayer of Conse-cration.

4   Saint Irenaeus, *Adversus haereses,* III,18,3; PG 7, 934.

5   Cf. *The Roman Pontifical,* "Ordination of a Bishop," Investiture with the Miter.

6   *Sources of Renewal: The Implementation of Vatican II,* London, 1980, p. 190.

7   *Liturgy of the Hours,* Fourth Sunday of Easter, Office of Readings, Responsory.

8   *The Roman Pontifical,* "Ordination of a Bishop."

9   Cf. *Liturgy of the Hours,* Office of Readings.

10 Ibid., Week XXIV, Monday.

11 Ibid., Week XXV, Friday.

12 Ibid., Week XXVII, Saturday.

13 Cf. Vatican Council II, *Decree on the Pastoral Office of Bishops in the Church*, 16.

14 Liebert J., *Poezje*, Warsaw, 1983, p. 144.

15 *The Roman Pontifical*, "Ordination of priests."

16 Apostolic Letter, *Rosarium Virginis Mariae*, 42.

17 Cf. the commentary on the "logo" on the cover of the *Catechism*.

18 *The Roman Pontifical*, "Ordination of priests."

19 Wolny J., *Księga Sapieżyńska*, Kraków, 1986, p. 776.

20 *Poezje i dramaty*, Kraków 1979, p. 230.

21 Wolny J., *Księga Sapieżyńska*, Kraków, 1986, p. 776.

22 Saint Augustine, *Sermo* 46,2; PL 38, 271.

23 Cf. *Code of Canon Law*, c. 276 §2,4°.

24 Boniecki A., *Kalendarium życia Karola Wojtyły*, Kraków, 2000, pp. 286–287.

25 Wyszyński S., *Zapiski więzienne*, Paris, 1982, p. 251.

26 Ibid., p. 94.

27 "Stanislas" 1–7, in Karol Wojtyła, *Poezje—poems*, Kraków, 1995, pp. 264–268.

28 *Pilgrimage to the Holy Places*, "3. The Identities."

29 "A Hill in the Land of Moriah," *Roman Triptych: Meditations*, trans. Jerzy Peterkiewicz, published by the U.S. Conference of Bishops, Washington, D.C., 2003.

BIBLICAL CITATIONS
AND MAGISTERIAL DOCUMENTS

NEW TESTAMENT

MAGISTERIAL DOCUMENTS

INDEX OF NAMES

Gorzelany, Józef, 80
Gregory the Great, Pope and Saint, 64
Groblicki, Julian, 182
Gromek, Maria, 96

Hedwig, Queen Saint, 21–22, 40, 195
Heydel, Zdzisław, 7, 8, 11, 23
Hlond, August, 7
Höffner, Joseph, 165
Husserl, Edmund, 90, 91

Ingarden, Roman, 90
Irenaeus, Saint, 33

James the Apostle, Saint, 4, 215
Janik, Jerzy, 88
Jankowski, Augustyn, 122
Jesus Christ, vii, ix, 3–5, 14–16, 24–27, 31–34, 35–37, 39, 40, 46, 48,
        49–50, 60–62, 64, 66–67, 69–71, 82, 90, 115, 116, 127, 129,
        138–42, 147, 153, 156–58, 162, 178, 179, 182, 183, 190, 197–99 ,
        211–16
Jeż, Ignacy, 138, 181
John XXIII (Angelo Roncalli), Pope, 151
John the Apostle, Saint, 4, 215
John of Kety, Saint, 196
John Paul I (Albino Luciani), Pope, 74
Jop, Franciszek, 30
Joseph, Saint, 137–40, 143, 144
Juan Diego (Cuauhtlatoatzin), Saint, 56

Kłósak, Kazimierz, 95
Kolbe, Maximilian, Saint, 198
Kominek, Bolesław, 30
Kotlarczyk, Mieczysław, 94
Kozal, Michał, 197
Kozłowiecki, Adam, 138
Koźmiński, Honorat, 119
Kuczkowski, Mikołaj, 59, 81, 97
Kurowski, Tadeusz, 163